Think Again

assembly material

by
Linda Hammond

To my parents

Acknowledgements

The author and publisher are grateful for permission to use the following copyright material:
'Little flower in the ground', words and music © Mayhew McCrimmon;
'When darkness creeps over the sea', words and music arrangement © Methodist Church Division of Education and Youth;
'We bring our gifts to the Lord', words and music © Mayhew McCrimmon;
'All this world belongs to Jesus', words © 1966 Willard F. Jabusch, St Mary of the Lake Seminary, Mundelein, Illinois 60060;
'When I needed a neighbour', words and music © Stainer and Bell Ltd;
'Haul, haul away', words and music © Mayhew McCrimmon.

Hammond, Linda
   Think again
   1. Schools — Exercises and recreations
   I. Title
   377′. 1   LB3015

ISBN 0–7197–0496–0

Artwork by Val Saunders

© Linda Hammond 1988

ISBN 0–7197–0496–0
Typeset by Avonset, Midsomer Norton, Bath
Printed in Great Britain at the University Press, Cambridge

CONTENTS

Think Again

Think again about the world you live in.
Think again about the things you do.
Think again of things you say,
   try and follow Jesus' way.
Think again and start your life anew!

Think again about each new beginning.
Think again of people that you see.
Think again and try and see
   there's a better way to be.
Think again, with Jesus life's complete.

Words and music: Linda Hammond

Something special

Seeds, which appear so dead, contain the source of new life. Given the right conditions, they will grow into plants in their own right.

Something special

In a small village, just this side of Duckton, there lived a man called Joe Webster. Now Joe had been born in the village. He had grown up in the village, worked in the village, and now he was growing old in the village. He knew everybody who lived there, and they all knew him — not only because he had been there so long, but because of his beautiful garden.

All day, every day, Joe would be out planting seeds, tending the new shoots, watering, hoeing, bedding out plants which he had grown in his greenhouse, or pruning the roses. In fact, he always did whatever needed doing straight away. The flowers and plants which grew in his garden were always strong and healthy, thanks to his loving care. When they looked at their best, Joe would choose them for something special.

Sometimes he would pick them to take into his own house, but more often than not he gave them away. Many people in hospital were cheered by being given some of his flowers. Old ladies enjoyed seeing and smelling them in Joe's garden and went home happily with a small posy. Children took them to school, and from time to time he delivered a large bouquet to Miss Wright so that she could use them to decorate the church for Sunday.

But this year, for some reason, something seemed to have gone wrong. Although the poppy and the snapdragon were looking their best, Joe didn't seem to notice them. Every time he came down the garden he chose some of the other flowers, and they were left behind.

Then one Friday night, there was a really strong wind — gates banged, dustbin lids were blown across the street, and branches were tossed to and fro. The next morning the two flowers looked very bedraggled. All their petals had been blown away, and who would want flowers without petals? But at that very moment, Mrs Anderson, who helped with the children on Sundays, was asking Joe if he had any flowers which had made seeds that she could show to the children. He gave her the poppy and the snapdragon.

Mrs Anderson showed them to her group of children. 'On Friday,' she said, 'these two stems had flowers, each with beautiful, coloured petals, but look at them now!'

'They're dead,' said a voice from the back of the room.

'No, Daniel,' replied Mrs Anderson. 'Although they may look it, they are not dead.'

Then Mrs Anderson took a knife and carefully cut across the ovary of each flower. She showed the children the small seeds nestling inside.

'Now what usually happens is that these seeds grow and ripen and then they are scattered by the wind. Some fall on hard, stony ground, some are eaten by birds, and some fall into soft soil, where they sleep through the winter. Then the following spring or summer they grow into new flowers. Now although these stems don't look very attractive at the moment, they are part of God's plan.' Mrs Anderson paused and smiled. 'God has a plan, or a special purpose, for each of us,' she said. 'But it may not always be what we think it should be. Sometimes we have to wait a long time to find out what it is.'

Then Mrs Anderson divided the seeds amongst the children and told them how to plant and care for them over the coming months.

It had seemed that the lives of the two flowers were over, but through their seeds they would live on, as constant reminders of God's love.

Activities

1   Read the parable of the sower in Mark 4.2-8. Compare it with the story and discuss.

2   Use the story to introduce the subject of old age. Joe Webster was an old man, but he was still able to create a beautiful garden, and make people happy with gifts of flowers. Ask the children to talk about any old people they know personally. Discuss what it means to get old, and the things that can be done to help make life easier for the elderly.

3   Mobility is very much a part of modern life. Families often move away from their roots and wider family. Make a large wall chart showing the geographical movements of each child's family.

4   Do a project on flowers.

   (a) Make a chart showing which flowers can be seen at different times of the year. Use bulb and seed catalogues.

(b) Cash in on colour:
  (i) List flowers of the same colour.
  (ii) Choose one flower, and then find other things which are the same colour.
  (iii) Use a flower to introduce an unusual colour, for example mauve.
  (iv) Ask children to bring items for a colour interest table.
  (v) Provide powder paints for the children to mix together and experiment with.

(c) Propagation:
  (i) Cut up flowers to show the children the seeds. Draw a very simple diagram of a flower and label different parts, eg petals, stamen, etc.
  (ii) Buy a packet of mixed seeds from a pet shop (gerbil food) and make a seed collage.
  (iii) Grow some mustard and cress on damp cotton wool.
  (iv) Plant some hyacinth or crocus bulbs in a pot to be kept in the dark ready for Christmas.

5 Discuss methods of seed dispersal — explosion, water, wind, birds and animals.

6 Go on an autumn treasure hunt looking for things such as sycamore seeds, conkers, acorns and beechnuts.

Prayer

Dear Father God,
        thank you for loving us and caring for us,
            as Joe loved and cared for his plants.

Help us to be patient when we have to wait for our turn to be chosen to do something special. It is not easy for us to stand by and watch as others are chosen first and we seem to be forgotten. Please help us to remember that one day we will be able to be useful, too.

Hymn

1 Little flower in the ground
   petals falling all around.
   Summer's past and autumn's here
   and now we know your end is near.

2 Seeds that fall on to the ground
   by the winds are scattered round.
   Some will feed the winter birds,
   and some will nestle in the earth.

3 Some will last the winter through
   'till the spring makes all things new.
   See the flower newly grown
   from seeds the winter wind has sown.

4 Praise the Lord in heav'n above,
   who shows us all the way of love.
   Praise him for the dying year.
   If winter comes then spring is near.

   Words: Michael Cockett
   Music: Kevin Mayhew

The unwelcome visitor

Homelessness, destitution and unemployment are problems which are with us today as they were a century ago.

The unwelcome visitor

Francis shivered, and pulled the ragged coat more tightly around his thin, hungry body. Huddled in a doorway, he watched the people of Plymouth hurrying about their business, oblivious of the very existence of Francis and the many urchins who — like him — only managed to survive by salvaging scraps of food from rubbish bins and by collecting discarded and often rotting fish from the harbour.

For months now, ever since his mother died, Francis had tried to find work. But times were hard, and even the ship owners, who were usually on the look-out for cheap casual labour, had more cabin boys and deck hands than they knew what to do with. If only his father would return from the sea, or at least send a message. Francis' eyes began to fill with tears.

'What you crying for?' inquired a voice.

'I'm not,' retorted Francis, quickly dragging the back of his hand across his face to remove the evidence, before he turned to see who had spoken to him.

It was Kit, a lad who had often joined him on scavenging raids in the past, but who had now come to persuade him that soft, tasty muffins from the bakery would be much better than the usual stale crusts. Francis was tempted — it was such a long time since he'd had any proper food. So as soon as it was dark, the two boys left the doorway and stealthily made their way along the gas-lit cobbled streets until they reached the bakery.

Darting inside, they hid behind some big sacks of flour until Francis thought it was safe to move. But the baker, who was still there, saw him.

'Stop, thief!' he shouted and made a lunge at Francis.

But hunger gave Francis speed and, grabbing a handful of muffins, he disappeared out into the night.

Now what was he to do? He knew it wouldn't be long before the constables tracked him down. Where could he go? Munching muffins, Francis looked round and noticed a small light going on and off at the far side of the harbour.

'That's it!' he thought. 'The new Breakwater Lighthouse. They'll never find me there!'

So he ran down to the harbour and slipped into the nearest rowing boat. He unfastened the mooring rope, picked up the oars, and headed out towards the light. When he got near the lighthouse, Francis let the boat drift slowly forwards until he could make out the landing stage. With a couple more pulls he reached it and tied up the boat. Then he walked up and knocked timidly on the big wooden door. There was no answer. He knocked again, shouted and kicked, and this time he succeeded in making someone hear.

Bill could hardly believe his eyes when he saw the small, bedraggled boy in front of him.

'What are you doing here?' he demanded. 'Don't you know it's not safe to be out at sea at night?'

Francis sniffed.

'I'm running away, Sir,' he said.

'Well, you can't stay here. A lighthouse is no place for a boy, apart from which it's against the rules to have ''unofficial visitors''! Do you want to get us into trouble?'

'Oh no, Sir,' Francis replied. 'I'll go, Sir.'

But as he turned to go back down the steps, there was a tremendous flash of lightning followed by a crash of thunder.

'Going to be a rough night, by the look of it,' said Bill. 'Perhaps you'd best wait till morning.'

Thankfully, Francis entered the lighthouse and heard the big door shut behind him. Bill handed him a mug of hot soup.

'Now you'd best tell me what you're running away from while you drink that,' he said.

'The constables, Sir,' was the ashamed reply.

'Oh, no!' groaned Bill. 'Not only are we breaking company rules having you here, but we're harbouring a criminal as well. What have you been doing?'

Hesitantly, Francis told him the whole story.

'Well, lad,' said Bill when he'd finished, 'we've a busy night ahead of us, so you'd best rest and we'll sort it all out in the morning.'

So saying, he tossed the boy a blanket and set off up the stairs to take his turn on duty with the lamp.

Tom, the other lighthouse keeper, was pleased to see him. It had been a long shift and he was tired.

'Any soup in the pot?' he asked.

'Well, there is a bit, but I gave some to our visitor,' replied Bill.

'Visitor?' Tom look puzzled.

Bill explained briefly.

'That's all we need!' said Tom crossly. 'A troublesome gutter-snipe!'

And he stomped out of the room, and down the stairs. Unfortunately, he was so busy thinking about the unwelcome visitor that he missed his footing, lost his balance, and fell head over heels to the bottom.

Francis woke with a start and sat up. Was it just thunder he'd heard? He got to his feet and walked unsteadily across the room. There, lying groaning at the bottom of the staircase was a man he'd not seen before. Realising that the man was hurt, Francis rushed up the stairs to get help. Round and round he went until he reached the top of the lighthouse.

'I'll go and see what I can do,' Bill told the breathless boy when he had explained. 'Meanwhile, you wait here and keep an eye on the light. If there's a problem, just shout!'

Half an hour later Bill was back. He'd made Tom as comfortable as possible, but he asked Francis if he'd sit with the injured man in case he needed anything in the night. Francis willingly agreed.

Next morning, although he was still afraid of being caught by the constables, Francis offered to take a message to the doctor in Plymouth.

'Thanks, lad,' said Bill, as he handed him the note. 'And here's tuppence three farthings so you can pay for the muffins.'

Gratefully, Francis wrapped the coins in his dirty hankerchief, tucked the letter inside his shirt and got into the bobbing boat. Perhaps the world wasn't such a bad place after all.

Footnote: The Plymouth Breakwater Lighthouse was built in 1844. It is now fully automated.

Activities

1   Lighthouses show sailors where there are rocks which should be avoided. Read what Jesus said about light in Matthew 5.14-16.

2   Francis, the boy in the story, had no home to go to. Play musical chairs, and point out that the child who is left out with no chair to sit on when the music stops is like a homeless person. Find out about homelessness in our own country today. Contact Shelter for information.

3 In the story, oil was burned in the lamp which made the light. Oil is a fuel, a source of power. Make a wall chart showing all the different sources of power that are available to us, using library books, etc, for reference.

4 Lighthouses are now being automated. Discuss, in very simple terms, automation and the effect it can have on people's working lives. 'Unemployment' is a word often heard today. Find out if the children know what it means.

5 Get the children either to talk or to write about what they would like to do when they are grown-up.

6 Do a project on the sea.

(a) It is not surprising that boats and shipping have been so important in the past since 71% of the earth's surface is covered by the waters of the oceans — the Atlantic, Indian, Pacific and Arctic. Other seas are in fact smaller, more self-contained parts of the oceans. Use this information to introduce the project, then ask the children to find out the names of some parts of the oceans. Discuss whether they are warm or cold, and what 'sea creatures', eg penguins, whales, sharks, flying fish or dolphins, they associate with each. A globe would be a valuable teaching aid.

(b) Obtain a tide table, and explain the variations.

(c) Give each child an outline map of the coastline of the British Isles so that they can mark in the various shipping areas. (See opposite page.) Record, or arrange for them to hear on the radio, one of the shipping forecasts so that they can follow it with their maps in front of them.

(d) When at sea, weather conditions are obviously very important. Make individual or class weather charts and keep a record for a period of at least two weeks. Encourage the children to use their own symbols, but suggest they make a point of watching a weather forecast on the television and note the symbols used.

(e) Since the year 1837, when Samuel Morse invented the Morse Code, sailors, lighthouse keepers and many others have used it to send each other messages. Ships in distress signal the letters SOS (save our souls) by radio or any other means available, for example sirens or hooters. The children may well wish to attempt to learn a few letters. They should remember that:

a dash is three times the length of a dot;
the time allowance between one letter or number and the next
is the length of about two dots;
the time allowance between words is a dash.
Then at least they can try to get it right!

A	.—	J	.———	S	...	1	.————
B	—...	K	—.—	T	—	2	..———
C	—.—.	L	.—..	U	..—	3	...——
D	—..	M	——	V	...—	4	....—
E	.	N	—.	W	.——	5	.....
F	..—.	O	———	X	—..—	6	—....
G	——.	P	.——.	Y	—.——	7	——...
H	....	Q	——.—	Z	——..	8	———..
I	..	R	.—.			9	————.
						0	—————

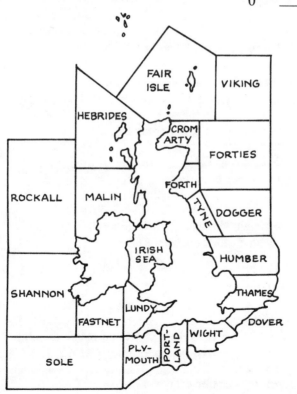

7   Do a project about lighthouses.

(a) Using maps and information obtainable from Trinity House, find out where British lighthouses are situated and whether they are fully manned, partially-manned or automatic. Record findings visually, for example by sticking small lighthouses on an enlarged outline of the British Isles in the appropriate places.
Trinity House
Tower Hill
London EC3

(b) Talk about the history of lighthouses, for example the Bell Rock — or Inchcape Rock — Lighthouse, built in 1811, which watches over the stormy seas around Inchcape in Scotland. Then have a story-writing session about a lighthouse.

(c) Arrange a visit to a lighthouse if there is one near enough, or obtain slides, films or videos on the subject.

(d) Teach the children a poem about a lighthouse such as the one that follows.

> Alone on the rocks I stand
> and watch the fishes play.
> Seagulls wheel and screech and dive
> and boats pass on their way.
> But then as moon replaces sun
> and twinkling stars appear,
> my light shines out all through the night
> to warn ships rocks are near.

(e) Make lighthouses.

Provide each child with:
two cardboard tubes, one to go inside the other;
sticky coloured-paper;
scissors;
felt-tip pens or crayons.

Method:

(i) Cut a window from near the top of the widest tube.

(ii) Put the longer, thinner tube inside, stand upright. Hold firm and draw outline of window on inside tube.

(iii) Remove the inside tube, cut and stick yellow paper over window outline.

(iv) Stick or draw a door, another window and some steps on the outside tube.

(v) Place the outside tube upright on a table and insert the inner tube so that the 'light' will shine through the window when the top is turned round.

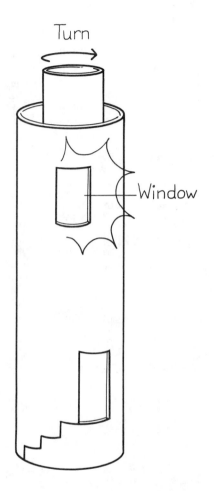

Turn

Window

Prayer

Teach us, Lord,
   always to look for the best, not the worst, in other people.
Teach us, Lord,
   to be like you, ready to give those who have done wrong another
   chance.
Teach us, Lord,
   to follow your example in everything we do.

Hymn

1 When darkness creeps over the sea
   and hides the far land from sight,
   what will the many ships do
   that seek their lone way through the night?
   Who'll guide them past the sharp rocks,
   who'll warn them danger is near,
   light up the darkness, with hope,
   banish the voyager's fear,
   and mark out the way?

2 The lighthouse-man comes to the task,
   to serve God and man through the night;
   climbs up his steep winding stair,
   his wonderful lamp sets alight;
   there, all alone, he keeps watch,
   flashing his lights o'er the waves,
   symbol of guidance divine,
   off'ring a service that saves,
   and showing the way.

3 Lord, when in the service of life
   we take up the tasks of our race,
   may we, like lightkeepers brave,
   be worthy our trust and our place;
   in the dark hours when men fail
   keep our faith burning and bright,
   lit by the flame of your love,
   Jesus, you heavenly light,
   our only true way.

Words: Robert Callin
Music: Mozart, adapted by Ida Buttle

16

God's harvest

Autumn is a wonderful season, the time for harvest thanksgiving.

God's harvest

Reading comics and watching cartoons on television can be fun. Sometimes they are serious, and sometimes they are funny. But, more often than not, there is someone or something that's good trying to win against someone or something that's bad. *(Ask for current examples.)*

Long ago, in the days before comics and television, people used to carve figures and paint pictures which told similar stories about good and bad. St George (who was good) killing the dragon (which was bad); God's angels (who were good) driving out the devil (who was bad).

In churches and cathedrals all over Europe, angels with haloes, trumpets and wings were shown to be winning in the fight against the devil, with his forked tail and two-horned head! These cartoon figures of the past were used to help people to understand that it wasn't always easy to follow Jesus' example and to do the right thing, especially if the devil was trying to tempt them to do wrong. But, as in the comics and cartoons of today, if those on the good side really tried hard, they usually won in the end.

So let's find out what happened one day when some school children were tempted to be bad, almost as if the devil had really got into them!

It was nearly nine o'clock on this particular morning, and children were streaming in through the school gates, carrying jars of jam, baskets of apples, boxes of eggs, tins of baked beans and spaghetti, bags of tomatoes and carrots, big, green cabbages, packets of biscuits and loaves of bread. They went down the corridors and into their classrooms, and in one room the children put the food on a big table near the window. Then they sat down in their places to do some number work. But they didn't stay sitting down for long.

Ben walked over to the big table and took some eggs to use as counters. He lifted them out of the egg box one by one and put them onto his workbook. The eggs started to roll, then they toppled over the edge of his desk — smash, smash, smash! What a mess they made on the floor. Mrs Johnson was very angry and couldn't understand what had made Ben do such a silly thing. Nor could she understand why somebody had taken bites out of all the apples!

Then Emma was caught dipping her finger into one of the jars of jam, and Tony and Lee got into trouble because they were playing marbles with the tomatoes. Poor Mrs Johnson didn't know what had got into the children that morning.

Even Nicola, who was usually so good, decided to help herself to the biscuits she had brought in earlier. She undid the paper carefully and began eating the biscuits one by one until there were none left at all. Then, just as she was chewing the last mouthful, Mrs Johnson looked up.

'What do you think you are doing, Nicola?' she asked sternly. 'Don't you know why you brought those biscuits to school today?'

'Yes, because it's harvest,' mumbled a tearful Nicola.

'Exactly,' said Mrs Johnson. 'And I think it's time we all had a chat about why we have a harvest service, after the things some of you have been up to this morning, don't you?'

As the children picked up the gifts they had brought with them, and lined up by the door ready to join the other classes who were waiting in the hall, Nicola started to cry again.

'What shall I do?' she said. 'I've eaten all the biscuits, so I haven't got anything to give to God.'

'Oh yes, you have,' said Mrs Johnson. 'You can give yourself. Everyone is part of God's harvest.'

As she spoke, they heard singing coming from the hall, so Mrs Johnson took hold of Nicola's hand and, together, they led the class in to join the rest of the school praising and thanking God for all the good things he provides.

Activities

1   Read a psalm of praise and thanksgiving for harvest, such as Psalm 65.9-13.

2   Do a comic survey. Collect old comics and let the children look through for examples of good triumphing over bad. Cut out those which are appropriate and display. Use these pictures to stimulate discussion on right and wrong.

3   Get the children to discuss current cartoon characters being seen on television. Children could act out situations, for example Tom, the

cat, trying to creep up and steal his master's dinner while Jerry, the mouse, tries to prevent him. This could easily be used as a game.

4   Visit an old church or cathedral to look at carvings, paintings and stained-glass windows.

5   Make 'stained-glass' windows.

Provide:
    thin card, with a 'window' cut out;
    sheets of different-coloured cellophane or tissue paper;
    scissors;
    glue.

Method:
    (i)   Cut out a piece of cellophane or thin paper, slightly larger than the 'window'.
    (ii)   Spread glue round the edge of the 'window', and press the 'glass' firmly into place.
    (iii) Tear or cut up different-coloured pieces of cellophane.
    (iv)   Put *little* spots of glue all over the 'window', and then carefully place the coloured cellophane as desired.
    (v)   Leave to dry.

6   Do a project on harvest.

(a) Start by asking the children to write down or discuss the food mentioned in the story.

(b) Choose one or two examples and follow the process through from 'field' to 'table'.

(c) Make and bake some biscuits, cake or bread. This introduces all sorts of mathematical concepts. Non-cook recipes are also fun to do, and may be easier to arrange.

Chocolate Fudgy Cups (makes approximately 30)

Provide:
    140 gm (5 oz) cooking chocolate;
    55 gm (2 oz) butter;
    3 drops vanilla essence;
    170 gm (6 oz) can sweetened condensed milk;
    115 gm (4 oz) icing sugar (sifted);
    1 level tablespoon cocoa;
    grated chocolate and vermicelli for decoration;
    paper cases.

19

Method:
- (i) Put chocolate and butter into a basin and place in a pan of hot water to melt.
- (ii) Remove basin from water.
- (iii) Add vanilla essence.
- (iv) Beat in condensed milk.
- (v) Sift icing sugar and cocoa together, then stir into the chocolate mixture.
- (vi) Beat until smooth and creamy.
- (vii) Fill paper cases with the fudge mixture.
- (viii) Decorate and leave in a *safe* place to cool.

Involve the children as much as possible in the weighing, counting, etc.

(d) Arrange a visit to a local bakery.

(e) Make play-dough:

> 2 parts flour;
> 1 part salt and water;
> food colouring and/or cooking oil can be added if required.

This can be used as a play material in its own right — for sharing, weighing and counting. Use it to make models for use either in the assembly or the classroom shop.

(f) Set up a shop, with empty cereal packets, egg boxes, plastic bottles, etc. Price items. Provide 'money' and encourage accuracy in making purchases. Discuss the place of origin and the use of individual items, for example, shoe polish from China.

Prayer

For all the good things we have to eat,
> jam, apples, eggs, baked beans, spaghetti, tomatoes, carrots, cabbages, biscuits and bread,
>> (*All*) we thank you, God.

For all the people who work so hard growing, preparing, packing, and bring the food ready for us to buy from the shops,
> farmers, bakers, factory workers and lorry drivers,
>> (*All*) we thank you, God.

For all the people who look after us, and earn money to buy food, or grow it for us to enjoy,
>mothers, fathers, aunts and uncles,
>>(*All*) we thank you, God.

For wanting all of us to be part of your harvest, even if we do naughty and silly things like the children in the story,
>>(*All*) we thank you, God.

Hymn

1 We bring our gifts to the Lord, our God. (Repeat)
2 We bring our love to the Lord, our God. (Repeat)
3 We bring ourselves to the Lord, our God. (Repeat)

Words and music: Estelle White

A night to remember

Bonfire night can be an exciting and enjoyable occasion or a tragic one, depending on whether safety precautions are taken and rules followed.

A night to remember

It was the fifth of November, the night when bonfires and fireworks are lit to remind us of Guy Fawkes who, a long, long time ago, was thought to have tried to blow up the Houses of Parliament in London.

Sally and Steven had no intention of blowing anything up, but they did enjoy having a bonfire. So as soon as they got home from school they rushed out into the garden to make a start. Steven raked all the fallen leaves together and then Sally loaded them into the wheelbarrow. In no time at all, there was a huge pile of leaves and twigs ready for Dad to burn later on.

Next they decided to make a Guy! Mum gave them one of their father's old suits, a large paper-bag and an old hat. Sally tied the bottom of each trouser-leg, and the wrist of each sleeve of the jacket with string, before they both set to work stuffing the suit with newspapers.

Poor old Guy! He did look strange without a head! So Steven drew a funny face on the paper bag with his felt-tip pens and then handed it to Sally to fill with paper. Together, they tied the head to the body and plonked the hat on top. The Guy was finished!

Now all they needed was their father, but they knew he wouldn't be home from work just yet, so they sat down to watch television while they waited.

Just after six o'clock, they heard his key in the door and ran to meet him.

'Hello, you two,' he said. 'What are you both so excited about?' As if he didn't know!

A few minutes later the family, wrapped up warmly from top to toe, went out into the garden. It was very dark, so as Steven was the only one with a torch, he led the way.

'Now,' said Dad. 'Before I do anything, I want you two to promise to stand well away from the fire and not come anywhere near while I light the fireworks, otherwise you might get hurt.'

'OK,' said the children.

They went and stood by Mum while their father lit the bonfire. Crackle, crackle, crackle — the leaves began to burn, and so did the Guy which Dad had put on top of the fire. How different the garden looked with the firelight casting flickering shadows on the nearby trees and bushes. Sally decided they looked like big, black monsters and snuggled up close to her mother.

Once the fire was going well, it was time for the fireworks. Dad took two out of the tin box and replaced the lid. Then he walked well away from the box and the children, and lit the fireworks carefully with a slow-burning taper. A gentle cascade of golden rain fell against the dark, night sky, followed by red, amber and green shooting stars, which Dad said were traffic lights. They did look pretty. The next firework was a rocket, which went zooming off high into the sky, followed by a Catherine wheel, which went round and round and round.

Their father gave Sally and Steven a sparkler each to hold while he prepared the next rocket for launching.

'Do you think it will reach the moon?' Steven asked.

His father laughed. 'No chance,' he said. 'The moon is far too far away.'

Steven was a bit disappointed. 'Perhaps if I gave it a helping hand,' he thought. Without realising how he got there, he found himself standing in front of the rocket.

Why didn't it go? The piece of paper at the bottom was still red. Steven bent down to take a closer look. He put out his hand.

'Steven! *No!*'

But the warning came too late. The rocket burst into life, burning Steven's hand as it reached for the stars. His mother hurried him indoors and quickly put the burnt hand into a bowl of cold water. Then she bandaged it up.

'Well, it could have been much worse, I suppose,' she said. 'But don't ever do anything so silly with a firework again!' Then she gave him a hug to show that she wasn't really cross, and they went back out into the garden.

Sally was watching Dad rake the baked potatoes out of the bonfire. They were wrapped up in silver paper. A few minutes later they were all standing eating the hot white insides of the potatoes with lots of butter. Steven found it rather difficult with only one hand, so he had to eat forkfuls given by the others.

'Well,' he thought to himself. 'What with making a guy, and having a bonfire, and a sparkler of my own, and seeing the fireworks, and eating baked potatoes out of the fire . . . what a night it has been!'

Then he looked down at his bandaged hand and felt the throb. 'But that is one thing I won't forget in a hurry.'

Activities

1 Find out all you can about the original Guy Fawkes and the plot to blow up the Houses of Parliament on 5 November, 1605.

2 Encourage the children to interpret this event artistically using brightly-coloured paint on black sugar paper. Add glitter.

3 Unfortunately, there are still people today who think problems can be solved by blowing things up. In 1984, the IRA planted a bomb at the Grand Hotel in Brighton in an attempt to kill the Prime Minister and other members of the government. Depending on age, talk to the children about major trouble-spots around the world, using current newspaper articles for reference and examples. Discuss the moral issues involved.

4 In the story, the trees and bushes were silhouetted by the light of the bonfire. Sometimes silhouettes can be seen in the moonlight. Discuss silhouettes with the children, and then set up a 'Profiles Studio'. One child stands between a painting-easel and a light-source (eg a slide-projector), so that the shadow of the profile is cast on the drawing paper. Another child, or an adult, then draws round the outline of the shadow with a black felt-tipped pen. The outline is then filled in with black paint.

5 Make toffee apples. Ask each child to bring an apple.
Provide:
    340 gm (12 oz) granulated sugar;
    170 gm (6 oz) golden syrup;
    55 gm (2 oz) butter;
    .45 litre (1/4 pint) water;
    red food colouring;
    1 lolly-stick per person.
This makes enough mixture to cover approximately eight medium-sized apples.
Method:
    (i)   Wash and dry the apples. Push a lolly-stick carefully into each apple at the stalk end.

(ii) *Adult to make syrup, or to supervise carefully.* Put water in a tall-sided, heavy saucepan and bring to the boil. Add sugar, syrup and butter and heat slowly, stirring all the time, until sugar dissolves and butter melts. Bring to the boil, cover, and boil gently for three minutes.

(iii) Uncover saucepan and continue to boil hard without stirring for eight to ten minutes. (Mixture is ready if a small sample separates into brittle threads when dropped from a wooden spoon into a cup of cold water.)

(iv) Move pan away from heat and add the red colouring. Approximately a teaspoonful per eight apples.

(v) Lift up each apple by the lolly-stick and dip into the hot toffee, swirling it round so that it is completely covered. Lift out and stand in a shallow, buttered tin. Leave until set cold.

(vi) If the apples are not going to be eaten straightaway, wrap each one separately in waxed or greaseproof paper.

6   Ask the children to make up their own firework code.

7   Do a project on space.

(a) Make a frieze showing some of the better-known planets and constellations, and real and imaginary spacecraft.

(b) Stimulate the children's imaginations by getting them to listen to a recorded selection of music from the Planet Suite by Holst.

(c) Play the game — 'When I went to the moon, I took with me . . . .'. Each child repeats what has already been said and adds his or her own suggestion, eg space helmet, moon buggy, oxygen, etc.

(d) Simulate mission control speaking to the crew in space. Provide the children with clean yoghurt pots, tins or plastic margarine tubs with holes pierced in the bottom, and lengths of string. Working in pairs, the children then thread the string between two identical containers, tying a knot firmly at both ends. When this string is pulled taut, they will be able to talk into one container and listen with the other.

(e) Instigate a search for information on space, with the children reporting back on what they can find. Record interesting items on a wall chart.

(f) Make a model space-station using odds and ends, including tinfoil, milk-bottle tops , cotton-reels, egg-boxes and egg-shells.

Prayer

Dear God,
    as we share this quiet time together, help us to remember the boy in the story who was hurt because he disobeyed the rules.

It is not always easy for us to understand the reasons for rules . . .
    . . . the reasons why we have to do things we don't want to do,
    and the reasons why we are not allowed to do some of the things we do want to do.

Please help us to be obedient when we are told to do something by people who love and care for us.

Hymn

26

1 Father, lead me day by day
   ever in your own good way;
   teach me to be pure and true,
   show me what I ought to do.

2 When in danger, make me brave;
   make me know that you can save;
   keep me safe by your dear side;
   let me in your love abide.

3 When I'm tempted to do wrong,
   make me steadfast, wise, and strong;
   and, when all alone I stand,
   shield me with your mighty hand.

4 When my work seems hard and dry,
   may I press on cheerily;
   help me patiently to bear
   pain and hardship, toil and care.

Words: John Page Hopps
Music: J B Calkin

Pulling together

Bellringing is one of the ways in which we celebrate Christmas.

Pulling together

Mark had always been fascinated by the big bells which hung in the church tower. Every Tuesday evening, as he lay in bed, he could hear them echoing through the darkness, as the ringers practised for Sunday. To Mark the sound was pure magic.

One day, on his way home from school, he noticed that the door at the bottom of the bell-tower was open. It was the chance he had been waiting for! Pausing only long enough to make sure that nobody was watching, he pushed open the little, iron gate into the churchyard, ran up the path and disappeared through the doorway.

Once safely inside, he looked around. But there wasn't much to see — only six, long ropes which hung through holes in the high ceiling and were then looped over hooks high on the walls.

'How boring,' thought Mark. Then he noticed a narrow, little, wooden staircase spiralling upwards in the corner which looked far more interesting. So up he went, round and round, until he reached the top. There, hanging in front of him, were six, huge bells — *his bells* — the ones he had listened to every Tuesday and Sunday for as long as he could remember. Gently, he put out his hand to touch the nearest bell . . .

'Oh no, you don't!' said a voice. 'Leave that bell alone!'

Mark was so frightened that he burst into tears. The owner of the voice clambered round the bell-frame towards him. Mark saw that it was Mr Taylor, the tower-captain.

'I'm sorry if I frightened you, young man,' he said. 'But you must never touch a bell or a bell-rope if you don't know how to ring. Bells are very valuable, and, what is worse, they can be dangerous and you could hurt yourself.'

Mark sniffed.

'Perhaps you'd like to tell me what you were doing,' said Mr Taylor kindly.

So Mark explained how much he had always loved the bells, and how he had seen the open door . . . one thing had led to another.

Mr Taylor looked thoughtful. 'In that case, why don't you to come and join us for a little while every Tuesday evening, and learn to ring a bell yourself?'

Mark's eyes lit up — there was nothing he would like better. And so it was arranged. Every Tuesday evening after that Mark went along to the tower for half an hour and learnt to ring. He had a special box to stand on because he was so much smaller than the grown-up ringers. First he learnt to ring a bell steadily on his own, and then he joined the other ringers. He learnt to wait and pull his rope in turn, so that the different notes of the bells came out in the right order. He also learnt that it was only by pulling together as a team that they could produce the music which rang out over the countryside.

Mark practised and practised, and longed for the day when Mr Taylor would say he was good enough to ring on Sundays.

The ringers worked as a team, so you can imagine the upset when Mr Johnson hurt his back and couldn't ring. Worst of all, it was Christmas Eve and there were extra services being held in church which meant extra bell-ringing. The only person who could have taken Mr Johnson's place had gone to spend Christmas with her daughter. What could they do?

Then Mr Taylor thought about Mark, and how hard he had been practising. So he telephoned Mark's mother, explained what had happened, and asked her if Mark could help out.

Two hours later, Mark found himself standing on his box with a bell-rope in his hand, waiting for the signal to start. Mr Taylor nodded at him, said the special words, 'Treble's going, she's gone', and they were off.

'Ding, dong, ding, dong.'

The bells rang out into the frosty night, inviting people to come and celebrate the birth of a very special baby.

'Ding, dong, ding, dong.'

Mr Taylor smiled encouragingly at Mark, who grinned back. His arms were beginning to ache, but he was happy because he knew he was doing his best, and that without him the team wouldn't be pulling together.

Activities

1 Use the episode in the story when Mr Taylor accidentally frightened Mark to introduce a class discussion on fear. This will need to be handled sensitively. Then provide paper and paints so that the children have a non-verbal medium through which to express some of these fears.

2　There are several accounts of people being frightened in the Bible. Ask the children to try to think of some examples, and to explain why these people were afraid. Follow this by telling or reading the Christmas story with special reference to the shepherds (Luke 2.1-20).

3　Provide an assortment of odds and ends for the children to turn into puppets — wise men, sheep, shepherds, a star, etc — and help them to put on a puppet nativity. (*The Know How Book of Puppets*, V Philpot, Usborne Publishing Ltd, is a useful source of ideas.)

4　Choose a Christmas poem that all the children can learn. Write it up in large letters on a piece of wallpaper, and stick the children's illustrations around the words.

5　Do a project on bells.

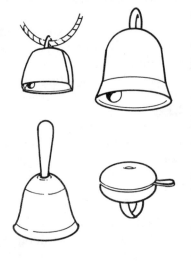

    (a) Make a wallchart of where bells can be found: churches; fire stations; schools; hotels; ships; bicycles; cat's collars; and so on.

    (b) Discuss when and why bells are rung, using pictures if possible. Examples could include church bells ringing for a wedding and cow-bells being used to prevent animals getting lost. Link the use of bells back to the town crier.

    (c) Find out as much as you can about bell-ringing and, if possible, arrange a visit to a bell-tower.

    (d) Make music using handbells, chime bars or improvised bottle-bells (different water-levels produce different pitches).

    (e) Set up a 'sounds' table.

    (f) Record different bell sounds on tape and ask the children to identify them.

    (g) Make Christmas-tree decorations like bells using egg-box segments, tinfoil, milk-bottle tops, glitter, etc.

Prayer

Dear God,
>we did not deserve your son, Jesus,
>>sent to us on the first Christmas day.

But you loved the world so much
>that you sent him to share the pain and the troubles,
>>the laughter and the joy.

Thank you, God, for the new life that came at Christmas.
>Thank you for Jesus,
>>and thank you for each Christmas day.

Hymn

1   Ding, dong! merrily on high
    in heav'n the bells are ringing.
    Ding, dong! verily the sky
    is riv'n with angels singing.

      Gloria.
      Hosanna in excelsis.

2   E'en so here below, below,
    let steeple bells be swungen,
    and io, io, io,
    by priest and people sungen.

3   Pray you, dutifully prime
    your matin chime, ye ringers;
    may you beautifully rhyme
    your evetime song, ye singers.

      Words: George Ratcliffe Woodward
      Music: Melody from Arbeau's Orchesographie

Think again

After Christmas we tend to feel flat and as if everything were over; but the message of goodwill is one for all time.

Think again

What excitement there had been in the weeks leading up to Christmas. Both at home and at school Kimberley had found herself caught up in a whirl of bustling activity — putting up decorations, making Christmas cards, shopping, hiding secrets, going to parties and, best of all, dressing up as Mary in the school play.

But now it was all over. Christmas day had been and gone. Aunty Sue and her family had returned home. All the Christmas cards had been taken down, and the decorations put away for another year. The Christmas tree, which just a few days ago had looked so beautiful with its tinsel and pretty lights, was now lying drab and discarded at the bottom of the garden. Dad had gone back to work, and Mum was busy trying to catch up on all the jobs which had been left over the holiday.

Kimberley looked out of the window. Even the weather seemed to reflect the feeling of gloom and despondency which had so quickly replaced the happy Christmas spirit of the previous weeks. The stark winter trees bent in the wind, as rain lashed against the glass. Kimberley could see old Mrs Smedley struggling along the pavement with a heavy load of shopping.

'Pity it's not sunny,' she thought. 'I'd be outside playing and then I could help her.'

The old lady stopped for a moment's rest, and as she did so, Kimberley remembered a song she'd once learnt called 'Think Again'. Why shouldn't she go and help? After all, she wasn't afraid of the wind and rain.

Kimberley had a quick word with her mother, then ran and opened the front door.

'Mrs Smedley, will you come in for a few minutes?' she called.

'Would you like a cup of tea?' Kimberley asked, as the old lady sank gratefully into a big armchair.

'Yes please, dear,' said Mrs Smedley. 'That would be lovely, if you're sure your mother won't mind.'

'Of course she won't,' replied Kimberley as she disappeared into the kitchen.

A few minutes later, Mrs Smedley was sipping her cup of tea.

'It's always the same this time of year,' she said. 'You'd think Christmas had never happened.'

'What do you mean?' asked Kimberley.

'Well, it's like this,' said the old lady. 'During December people try really hard to be nice to each other. They give cards and presents to friends and relations and even wish complete strangers a "happy Christmas". You children have all sorts of special treats at school, and parents spend a great deal of time and money trying to make you happy. Old people like me, who live alone, are visited by lots of well-wishers and invited to a lovely Christmas lunch. Then, as soon as Christmas day is over, it's as though we never existed; no visitors, no nothing.'

Mrs Smedley could see that Kimberley didn't really understand, so she continued.

'People get so wrapped up in themselves and their own ideas that they forget to think about other people and how they can help them. Mind you, this awful weather doesn't do much to encourage kindness. Have you ever noticed that sunshine can have a Christmas effect on people?'

'You mean people are nicer to each other?' queried Kimberley.

Mrs Smedley nodded.

'That's about the size of it, dear, so roll on the summer! Now, if you don't mind, it's time I was on my way.'

While Mrs Smedley eased her way out of the chair, Kimberley went to find her mac and wellies and to tell her mother what she was doing.

'I won't be long,' she called as she opened the front door.

For a moment, the girl and the old lady stood watching as a brilliant shaft of sunshine broke through the overcast sky, making the wet pavement glisten in front of them. Mrs Smedley winked.

'I feel better already,' she said, smiling, as she and Kimberley started the slow walk home.

Activities

1   Ask the children if they can remember whose birthday it was a few weeks ago (Jesus'), then compare Christmas celebrations with

traditional birthday celebrations, eg Christmas cards/birthday cards, Christmas presents/birthday presents, Christmas parties/birthday parties, Christmas cake/birthday cake, Christmas treats/birthday treats.

2   Follow up this discussion by asking the children to draw some of the presents they received, and also what they would have given Jesus if he had been born today.

3   Set up a 'what babies need' interest table.

4   Arrange for a willing and able mother to demonstrate bathing and dressing a baby in the classroom. Use this to emphasise how much looking-after babies need.

5   Invite the children to bring in photographs of themselves as babies. Mix the photos up, and see how many can be correctly identified.

6   Ask the children to compile their own family trees, using a combination of photographs and their own drawings. Encourage them to see that every family tree is different and that the differences are to be enjoyed, not hidden.

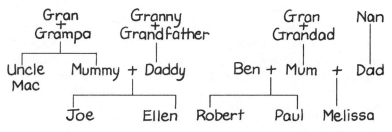

7   Although there are no photographs of Mary, Joseph and Jesus (ask the children to suggest why not), there are hundreds of pictures of them. Some show what is called the flight into Egypt. Because Joseph was warned of danger, he had to 'think again'. Ask the children to read, or read to them, the account of what happened in Matthew 2.13-15.

8   Do a project on the sun.

(a) Egypt, where Mary and Joseph took Jesus, is a hot country with plenty of sun. Discuss what happens if there is too much sun and no rain, and — if possible — demonstrate as follows. Fill a baking tray with soil. Add a few growing weeds. Put the tray into a lighted oven for a few minutes, or a hot cupboard or boiler room

35

for a few days, and show the children what happens. A damp cloth held under a hot light bulb can be used to show evaporation.

(b) Use these practical demonstrations to introduce the children to one of the particular problems of many developing countries — drought. Encourage them to find out about irrigation schemes. Obtain Oxfam's Schools and Youth Materials Catalogue. *Disasters in the Classroom* might be a particularly useful teaching pack to buy.

> Oxfam
> 274 Banbury Road
> Oxford OX2 7D2

(c) Using a piece of hardboard as a base, help the children to construct a model of an agricultural village in a developing country with a hot climate. Use this to help the children to understand how many people in these countries make skilful use of local materials to construct houses suitable to the climate and to their needs. Papier mache, clay, twigs and leaves, and junk materials could all be used.

(d) Give the children old holiday brochures to cut up and make into a montage. Help them to compare the Third World view of the sun as a potential enemy with that of many people in the affluent West who just enjoy sunbathing.

(e) Increase the children's awareness of the importance of the light and warmth of the sun for all aspects of life as we know it by giving them beans to grow in jam jars, between sheets of damp blotting paper.

Method:
    (i)   Leave some jars in daylight and put a few away in a dark place.
    (ii)   When those in the light start growing, leave most in the sunshine, but put a few in the fridge.

Discuss what happens, and why, relating this to the importance of the sun.

(f) Let the children divide pieces of paper in half — day and night — and draw pictures of what they do during each half of the day.

(g) Check that the children know about the 24 hour clock. Then introduce the idea of telling the time by the sun, using a sun-dial. If the weather is suitable, go and see a sun-dial locally.

Prayer

Ask the children to have their ideas ready.

Dear God, help us to think again about the world in which we live . . .
eg beauty, nature, homes, poverty.

Help us to think again about the things we do . . .
eg playing fair, being honest, helping others.

Help us to think again about the things we say . . .
eg not telling lies or swearing, remembering to say 'thank you'.

Help us to think again about each new beginning . . .
eg school, recorder or swimming lessons, day.

Help us to think again about the people we meet . . .
eg other people's needs, helping.

Help us to think again about the way we live and try harder to follow your example.

Hymn

1 Dear master, in whose life I see
   all that I would, but fail to be,
   let your clear light for ever shine,
   to shame and guide this life of mine.

2 Though what I dream and what I do
   in my weak days are always two,
   help me, oppressed by things undone,
   Jesus, whose deeds and dreams were one!

   Words: John Hunter
   Music: S Stanley

Skating for gold

It's tempting to show off when you are good at something. But that kind of pride and self-satisfaction doesn't always have the desired results.

Skating for gold

Joanna was a show-off. There was nothing she liked better than whizzing across the ice, wearing her white boots and a pretty, sequinned dress. Leaps, turns and spins were accomplished with ease, and if any less competent skater should dare to cross her path there was usually trouble.

'Out of my way, tortoise!' she would shout rudely. 'This is an ice-rink, not a lettuce-patch!'

So it was hardly surprising that nobody liked her, and that most of the other skaters avoided practising with her as much as possible.

Month after month passed as Joanna continued to dazzle the onlookers and upset the other children, until things came to a head at the 'Hardington Ice Olympics'. This was a competition organised each year by the management of the ice-rink to encourage all their young skaters to reach a higher standard. Joanna was delighted to have the opportunity to show off before such a large crowd, and was convinced that she would win the gold medal. In fact, she was so confident that she was overheard telling the other girls that she couldn't understand why they were even bothering to enter the competition, as they didn't stand a chance!

As the great day got nearer Joanna spent as much time as she could practising, while her mother anxiously put the finishing touches to the beautiful, new, rainbow dress which her daughter was to wear. At last everything was ready, and all the boys and girls who were taking part sat chatting nervously to each other as they awaited their turns.

Mr Morris announced their names, and then, as the music started, each young hopeful glided on to the ice, to be rewarded when they finished by enthusiastic applause.

Joanna waited impatiently. It was her skating they should be clapping. Then it was her turn.

'I'll show them,' she thought, as, slowly at first, then gathering speed, she glided across the rink. After a graceful turn, she leapt high into the air, flinging her arms wide.

That was when it all started to go wrong. There was an ominous tearing sound, as Joanna felt the shoulder seams of her dress come apart. Frantically, she tried to hold the material together, and lost her concentration. Doing a spectacular somersault en route, she canoned straight into the side of the rink. How the crowd and the other skaters laughed as they watched 'Little Miss Stuck-up' come unstuck. In tears, Joanna struggled to her feet and left the ice.

When she reached the changing-room, she sat down and buried her head in her hands. If only she hadn't been such a show-off, the accident might never have happened . . . If only she hadn't been so unkind, maybe one of the other girls would have lent her a dress so that she could have finished her programme . . . If only . . . Now she'd never even win the bronze medal, let alone the gold.

Poor Joanna was so upset that she didn't notice the changing-room door open, and a small figure sit down beside her. It was Kamla, a fairly new skater. Joanna had often made fun of her during the practice sessions.

'Are you all right?' she enquired anxiously.

Joanna looked up in surprise.

'Yes, thanks,' she sniffed. 'Nothing's broken — only my dress.'

'I was wondering . . .' Kamla said rather hesitantly. 'Would you like to borrow mine?'

Joanna could hardly believe her ears. Kamla was offering to lend her her dress.

'Do you really mean it? ' she asked.

'Yes,' replied Kamla. 'You're such a good skater. It would be a pity if the judges never saw what you can do.'

Joanna hugged her.

'Thanks,' she said. 'I'll never forget this.'

Then she dashed out of the changing-room to go and find Mr Morris and ask him if she could try again.

Half an hour later, Joanna was back on the ice, a rather different figure. No longer the conceited show-off in a flashy dress, but a talented skater in borrowed clothes. This time the applause was loud and long for the courageous girl who had come back to have another go, and who, maybe, might win the gold medal next time.

Activities

1   Read the passage in Matthew 6.5-8 where Jesus is telling us not to be

40

like the people who 'show off' by saying their prayers in places where they know they will be seen. Talk about this in relation to the story.

2 Ask each child to write a short prayer to God saying sorry for something he or she has done which hurt someone else.

3 As Joanna, the girl in the story, was very concerned about her appearance, she probably spent a lot of time looking in the mirror. Give the children a selection of mirrors and other reflective materials with which to experiment. Include water. Explain the refraction of light which causes a drinking straw to appear to bend when it enters the water, and ripples distorting the image reflected. Discuss with the children.

4 Try mirror painting.

Provide:
    protective clothing;
    a flat newspaper-covered surface on which to work;
    thickly-mixed powder-paints in bright colours;
    a large sheet of white paper.

Method:
    (i)   Fold the paper in half, then open it out and lay it flat.
    (ii)   Drip blobs of paint on to one half of the paper only.
    (iii) While the paint is still wet, quickly fold the clean half of the paper over the painted one and press it down hard.
    (iv)   Open up the paper, and you will find that the paint has blotted into a mirrored pattern. Both halves now match each other exactly.

5 Do a project on winter sports.

(a) Ask the children what they understand by 'winter sports'. Broaden their knowledge and understanding of the subject using maps and pictures illustrating where people go to do winter sports and the kind of specialist clothing and equipment needed.

(b) Winter sports involve both snow and ice.

Show the children some half-frozen ice cubes so that they can see the crystal formation. Let them watch the cubes melt and then refreeze them.

Give each child a piece of white paper. Show how this can be folded in half diagonally, then in half again, and pieces cut or torn

41

from each edge to make snowflake patterns. More folds can be made. These 'snowflakes' should be glued on coloured paper for dramatic effect.

Make 'snowy' finger-paint for the children to decorate windows or mirrors. Mix white powder-paint with a little flour, melted sugar, silver or white glitter, salt and water.

(c) Organise an 'ice' hockey match on a smooth, splinterless floor with the players in socks and a bean-bag being used in place of a puck. This should be supervised carefully.

(d) Once every four years the Winter Olympics are held. Sportsmen and women from all over the world compete for bronze, silver and gold medals. Discuss whether this and other forms of competition are a good idea.

(e) Make medals, using milk-bottle tops, etc. These should then be distributed fairly amongst the children.

Prayer

God, thank you for the gift of our bodies,
    which enable us to do so many different things . . .
    children's suggestions.

Remind us not to take our bodies for granted,
    but to look after them properly.

Help us to play fair
    when we use our bodies to compete with others.

Keep us from boasting
    when we win.

Keep us from moaning and making excuses
    when we lose.

Please help us so to live
    that our minds and bodies may be well.

Hymn

1 Take my life, and let it be
consecrated, Lord, to thee;
take my moments and my days,
let them flow in ceaseless praise.

2 Take my hands, and let them move
at the impulse of your love;
take my feet, and let them be
swift and beautiful for thee.

3 Take my voice, and let me sing
always, only, for my King;
take my lips, and let them be
filled with messages from thee.

4 Take my love; my Lord, I pour
at your feet its treasure-store;
take myself, and I will be
ever, only, all for thee.

Words: Frances Ridley Havergal
Music: W H Havergal

A world full of hope

However little you have, sharing can bring pleasure to you and others.

A world full of hope

How would you like to have been born 150 years ago? You've never thought about it? Well, it wouldn't have been so bad if your parents had a lot of money. But if they hadn't much money, then you would probably have been sent out to work to help earn enough to buy food for the family. This might have meant working long hours in a hot, crowded factory, or crawling through narrow tunnels in a mine, or climbing up inside big, dirty chimneys to clean them. And to make matters worse — there were no such things as holidays. It was not surprising that Sam and Dick got fed up!

All day, every day — and sometimes well into the night — Sam and Dick cleaned chimneys. Then one day they decided that enough was enough. It would be better to run away!

Just as they were, covered in soot from head to toe, they ran through the narrow, cobbled streets of the town, towards the canal. They were in luck. A heavily-loaded barge was moored at the wharf. Moving quickly and quietly, they lifted the tarpaulin cover and wriggled out of sight.

Minutes later they heard the sound of footsteps coming along the tow-path. Fortunately, the man was far too busy harnessing his horse to notice the two extra bumps of cargo. As soon as the horse was harnessed up, the man undid the mooring rope and gave the word. Very slowly, the barge began to move along the canal.

'I'm hungry,' whispered Dick. 'You got anything to eat?'

'Don't think so,' whispered back Sam.

But as he felt in his holey pockets, his fingers touched something hard. It was a sooty, half-eaten apple.

'You have it,' he said softly, offering it to his friend, although he, too, was very hungry. 'After all, I had the other half!'

After a while, lulled by the soothing sounds of horse's hooves and lapping water, the two boys fell asleep. The barge journeyed slowly onwards towards the sea.

Many miles — and some hours — later, they awoke to find they were no longer moving. Dick peeped out from under the tarpaulin to see what was happening. Two men, both leading horses, were having a fierce argument on a small bridge. Each wanted to cross, as this was the place where the tow-path changed sides, but neither man would give way to the other. One of the men was from the barge Dick and Sam were in.

'I think this is a good time for us to get off,' said Dick.

So the two boys began to slide out from under the cover. But just at that moment, the man from their barge looked up and saw them. Leaving his horse on the bridge, he ran back along the tow-path as fast as he could and arrived just in time to grab Dick and Sam by the scruffs of their necks.

'And what might you two ragamuffins be doing?' he roared.

'N-nothing, Sir,' stuttered Sam. 'We was only having a ride, Sir. We wasn't doing no harm — honest, Sir!'

Looking at the boys' dirty, frightened faces, the bargee's grim expression softened a little. He let them go, and told them to sit down.

'Now, tell me what's going on,' he said.

Little by little, as the story unfolded, Charlie — for that was the bargee's name — began to understand how hard things had been for Sam and Dick and why they had run away.

'Well, not that I agrees with running away, mind,' he said, 'but if the pair of you'd like to come along with me for a bit, I wouldn't say no. I don't have much, mind, but I'd be happy to share what I do have for the sake of a bit of company.'

Suddenly Charlie looked up.

'Oh no!' he shouted. 'I forgot all about Betsy! Where can she be?'

Sam and Dick gazed around, bewildered.

'My horse,' Charlie shouted in explanation as he ran up the tow-path. 'None of us will be going nowhere without her!'

Later that evening, with Betsy safely tethered alongside, two somewhat cleaner, and (for the first time in their lives) well-fed boys sat at the front of the barge with Charlie. They found it difficult to believe all they could see: green, open countryside instead of narrow, dirty, cobbled streets; masses and masses of sky, decorated with shining stars, instead of rows of roofs and chimneys. It was a new world to Sam and Dick — a beautiful world, a world full of hope, a world to look forward to living in, and a world to be happy in.

Charley smiled to himself as he guessed what they must be thinking. He was going to enjoy sharing it with them, too!

Activities

1 Talk to the class about what it must really have been like living 100 or 150 years ago. Arrange to visit a local museum if there is one which includes material on everyday life in the 19th century.

2 In the story, Sam and Dick had to clean chimneys. Discuss how this is done today. Conduct a survey to find out what proportion of houses in the area still have chimneys today. Find out how many of the children have open fires at home.

3 Do a project on canals.

   (a) Introduce the children to the project by looking with them at maps of the area to see if there are any canals in the vicinity. If so, arrange a visit, discussing beforehand rules for ensuring safety on and around canals and rivers. If not, obtain brochures on canal holidays for the children to look at.

   (b) Find a map which shows a canal or, even better, several canals. Photocopy so that each child can colour in the canals.

   (c) Discuss the differences between rivers and canals. Explain why canals were built.

   (d) Flat-bottomed barges were used to carry cargo along the canals. Make model barges. Empty date-boxes are ideal in shape, but the polystyrene trays in which meat is packed in supermarkets can also be used. Float the model barges, and experiment by loading different things into them.

   (e) Demonstrate and explain how a canal lock works.

   (f) Help the children to find out how a horse was used to pull a barge along a canal, by joining in this practical demonstration.

      (i) Mark out, with chalk or string, two parallel lines on the floor with a gap in between to represent the canal.

      (ii) Three children stand in the canal, in a line, with their hands on the shoulders of the child in front. They are the barge. The front child holds on to one end of a short rope or string. The other end of the rope is taken by another child who is the horse on the bank. The horse is led by another child on the bank who is the bargee. Six other children stand in pairs on opposite banks holding hands across the canal. They are the bridge.

(iii) Now tell the children what happened when the canal went under a bridge, or when the tow-path changed from one side of the canal to the other. Get them to act out these situations.

Sometimes the horse could walk under the bridge on a very narrow tow-path if the path stayed on the same side of the canal.

Sometimes the bargee would undo the rope and lead the horse over the bridge when the tow-path changed sides.

Sometimes a canal went under a very low bridge, and the bargee would take the horse over the bridge first, and then return to his barge and 'walk' it through. This meant lying on his back on the barge roof and using his legs to push against the ceiling of the bridge to move the barge along.

(g) Restore order by asking the children to draw a simple picture of a barge on a canal, including the tow-path and a bridge.

4   Ask for suggestions of stories in the Bible which are about sharing. One of the children may mention the feeding of the five thousand. Read in Mark 6.30-44 about the sharing of the loaves and fishes and then discuss the story.

5   Involve the children in sharing activities, including dividing an apple and naming the divisions, ½, ¼, ⅛, etc.

6   Do apple printing.

Provide:
> protective clothing;
> thickly-mixed powder-paint;
> paint brushes;
> folded or squared paper;
> halved apples.

Method:
(i)   Brush paint over the cut surface of the apple.
(ii)   Push it down firmly on the squared paper.
(iii)   Remove the apple carefully so as not to smudge the print.
(iv)   Print different colours in alternate squares.

Prayer

Dear God,

it is easy for us to think that all people are just as lucky as we are. Most of us take it for granted that we will have warm homes to live in, plenty of food to eat, and people who love and care for us.

But some children don't have everything they need — even here in . . . *insert the name of the town or area to which the children belong.*

In poorer countries, many, many children don't enjoy all these things we take for granted. Help us to remember this, and show us how we may share some of what we have to give others a world full of hope.

Hymn

1 All this world belongs to Jesus,
   everything is his by right;
   all on the land, all in the sea;
   everything is his by right.

2 Shining stars in all their beauty
   are outnumbered by his gifts.
   Sand on the shore, stars in the sky,
   are outnumbered by his gifts.

3 Every foot that starts a-dancing
   taps a rhythm full of hope;
   full of his joy, full of his hope,
   taps a rhythm full of hope.

4 All that's good reflects his goodness;
   may it lead us back to him.
   All that is good, all that is true,
   may it lead us back to him.

5 So give thanks for what he's given;
   touch and taste, and feet to dance;
   eyes for the lights, ears for the sound,
   for the wonders of our Lord.

Words: Willard M Jabusch
Music: Traditional Westerwald Melody

Old Reuben's donkeys

Jesus came into Jerusalem riding on a donkey. The Palm Sunday story would lose its meaning if he had come in any other way.

Old Reuben's donkeys

Nothing exciting ever seemed to happen in the little village near Bethphage where Elisheba lived with her parents and her brother, Jamin. Days passed, weeks passed, years passed — but little changed beneath the flat roofs of the small, white houses that snuggled against the hillside or in the dusty tracks that wound between them. The grown-ups worked from morning to night, the children helped when they could (and played when they couldn't), and the animals munched their way through the long, warm days.

On this particular morning, Elisheba had volunteered to take the pitcher to the well to get some water. It was a job she enjoyed doing, because it gave her the chance to get out of the house and see her friends. Sure enough, gathered around the well she found Ruth, Mehetable and Hannah, her brother Jamin, and the usual crowd of boys. But what, she wondered, were they all so excited about this morning?

As she got nearer, she could see them pointing in the direction of the track which led through the olive trees from the main Jericho road. Two strangers were walking quickly towards the village — their village. But who could they be, and where had they come from?

Like a swarm of locusts, the children descended. They besieged the strangers with questions, one following another so quickly that there was no time for answers. Gradually the noise subsided, then one of the men asked if any of the children had seen a donkey anywhere.

What a silly question! Of course they had! Without further ado, the children led the two men through the narrow village streets to old Reuben's yard.

'There she is,' they shouted, pointing to a donkey in the corner. 'But you'd better watch out. Old Reuben doesn't like people messing about with his donkey or her foal.'

'Don't worry,' said the taller of the two men. 'We have to take the donkey, but we aren't going to harm her or her foal. We'll take good care of them.'

While he spoke, the other man was undoing the rope which tied the two donkeys to a wooden post.

Just then, an elderly man came shuffling into the courtyard. It was old Reuben. He was more than a little surprised at the scene which met his eyes — crowds of children, and two strange men who were about to make off with both his donkeys!

'Hey! Just a minute!' grumbled old Reuben. 'What do you think you are doing with my donkeys?'

The strangers gave the reply which they had been told to give if challenged.

'Our master needs them and will send them back straight away.'

They were very relieved when old Reuben seemed satisfied by their answer, and they began to lead the donkeys away. But the children wanted to know more.

'Who is your master?' asked Jamin.

'And what does he want old Reuben's donkeys for?' piped up his sister.

The men told them that their master was a man called Jesus, but they didn't really know why he wanted the donkeys.

'Why don't you help us take them to Jesus, then you'll find out for yourselves,' suggested one. 'I'll bring you all back later on.'

Excited shouts greeted this idea, and so it was that a small procession made its way from the village towards the place where Jesus was waiting with his other disciples on the road just outside Bethphage.

When the donkeys had been safely delivered, Jesus explained that he was going to ride the young one into Jerusalem. He would fulfil a prophecy — 'Here is your king, who comes to you in gentleness, riding on an ass, riding on the foal of a beast of burden.' Although neither the disciples nor the children really understood what he meant, they were eager to do what they could to help. The disciples put their cloaks on the young donkey's back and then helped Jesus to mount. Elisheba broke a branch from a nearby bush and used it to keep the flies away from Jesus' face while he sat waiting until everything was ready.

Then everyone was ready, and the procession began to move slowly towards Jerusalem. At first, just the disciples and the children from Bethphage followed Jesus. Then, gradually, more and more people came to see what was going on. When they realised it was Jesus, they threw their cloaks down in the road in front of him, and cut down branches from the trees to wave. They cheered him on his way, shouting 'Hosanna to the

Son of David! Blessings on him who comes in the name of the Lord! Hosanna in the heavens!' And then they followed on at the tail of the procession.

On and on they all went, singing and chanting their praises until the triumphant procession finally reached Jerusalem. By this time the children were really tired, so the tall disciple who had come with them all the way from Bethphage let them have a rest and found them something to eat. Then he collected old Reuben's donkeys and walked with the children all the way back to their little village — the village where nothing exciting ever happened and nothing ever changed.

But something exciting had happened that day, and something had changed. They had met Jesus, and things would never be the same again.

Activities

1   Look up the events of Palm Sunday in Matthew 21.1-11. Read and compare with the story of old Reuben's donkeys. (Quotes used in the story are taken from the *New English Bible*.)

2   Make palm branches from rolled newspaper or crepe paper.

3   Decorate the classroom with a frieze, eg *Palm Sunday and Easter Day Frieze*, published by NCEC.

4   Encourage the children to use Bibles to find out what happened to Jesus after he arrived in Jerusalem. Was everybody pleased to see him? (Matthew 21.15, 45-46) If not, why not?

5   Follow up this research with a simple, matter-of-fact account of the events of Holy Week, with the emphasis on Easter Sunday. (Matthew 26.14 to 28.20)

6   Provide painting materials so that each child can express what he or she imagines took place in the garden that first Easter morning.

7   Do a project on donkeys.

   (a) Ask the children to suggest why Jesus chose to ride on a donkey, rather than a horse, when he went to Jerusalem. Discuss. (Donkeys, as beasts of burden, symbolise humility, whereas horses, used for military purposes, symbolise pride and conquest.)

(b) Use this outline to make a template of a donkey. Draw round it to provide each child with an outline. They should colour or decorate these, using paint or pens or collage. Display the donkeys in an imaginative way.

(c) Teach the children a poem about a donkey, such as this one.

> Little donkey standing,
> waiting in the sun.
> On his back a heavy load,
> he'll work till day is done.
> Trudging, trotting, walking,
> along each narrow track,
> he won't groan or grumble
> at the burden on his back.
> He's far too busy dreaming
> of the day not long ago,
> when two men came to take him
> to a place he did not know.
> They put their coats upon him,
> and then Jesus had a ride
> into the holy city
> on a donkey filled with pride.
> As the shouts rang out — 'Hosanna' -
> in the happy donkey's ears,
> he knew that he'd remember this
> for years and years and years.

(d) Let the children see a picture of a donkey which shows clearly the markings of a cross on its back. Or, even better, let the children see a real donkey if that is possible. Find out if the children think the marks on a donkey's back are there because a donkey carried Jesus into Jerusalem.

(e) Ask the children to tell you where we see donkeys in this country. Suggestions may include on the beach, at summer fetes, on children's farms, or in races run by local charities. Organise some races, letting the children pretend to be donkeys.

(f) Ask the children if they know what donkeys like to eat. Carrots! Invite them to bring carrot tops from home. If placed in shallow water, these should start to shoot.

(g) Play at pinning the tail on the donkey. A large picture of a donkey, a separate tail and a blindfold will be needed. Instead of the blindfold individual having to find the right spot on his own, ask another child to provide instructions, for example: take three steps left; four steps forward; feel the top of the board; follow the edge to the right; down a bit; left at bit; etc. This then becomes an exercise in co-ordination, co-operation and trust.

Prayer

Lord, as we stand here quietly for a few minutes, let us think again about the story of Palm Sunday.

> We are glad you chose to ride into Jerusalem on the back of a donkey.
> We are glad the children and grown-ups were able to see you and wave to you.
> We are glad they shouted 'Hosanna'.

It would have been lovely to have been there ourselves all those years ago and cheered you on your way, but we weren't there.

A week later you died and then came back to life. So you are here with us now — watching us wave our pretend palm branches and listening to our real 'Hosannas'.

Thank you, God, for coming into the world and sharing it with us.

Hymn

1 Give me joy in my heart, keep me praising,
give me joy in my heart, I pray.
Give me joy in my heart, keep me praising.
Keep me praising 'till the end of day.

Sing hosanna! Sing hosanna!
Sing hosanna to the King of Kings!
Sing hosanna! Sing hosanna!
Sing hosanna to the King!

2 Give me peace in my heart, keep me resting . . .

3 Give me love in my heart, keep me serving . . .

Words and music: Traditional

Not me

If Easter is just 'the day when we get Easter eggs', then waiting for Easter day can prove difficult.

Not me

Have you ever noticed that time always seems to go much more slowly when you want it to go fast?

That was Patrick's trouble. There were still two, long days to wait for his Easter eggs, and he was tired of waiting! He had often wondered why Easter Sunday had been chosen as the day for giving Easter eggs, and not Good Friday, which came first. It was probably just grown-ups being mean! Today was Good Friday, but Patrick certainly did not feel like being good. What could he do to while away the time?

He went into the bathroom, and saw the tube of toothpaste on the shelf.

'People decorate their windows for Christmas — so why not for Easter?' he thought.

He picked up the toothpaste and began to squeeze the tube. Soon there was a squiggly pattern all round the bathroom window. It did look pretty!

But his mother did not think so when she found it a couple of hours later.

'Who did this?' she asked angrily.

'Not me,' said Patrick.

'Well, it definitely wasn't Ian, he's been out playing all morning. So you'd better help Mr Nobody clear up!' she retorted.

She handed Patrick a cloth and went back downstairs to finish getting the lunch.

As soon as they had finished eating, Patrick and Ian asked their mother if they could go outside to play. When she said 'yes', they grabbed their anoraks and wellies and charged out through the kitchen door into the garden.

'Who left the door open?' their mother called after them.

'Not me,' shouted Patrick from half-way up the nearest tree. Of course it was Patrick really, but he was not going to climb down just to shut a door!   After a little while, Ian went in to watch television. Once again, Patrick couldn't think of anything to do. He wandered into the shed, and then he saw Dad's cupboard. He opened the door, and there — just waiting for him — was the tool-box. Patrick lifted the lid and took out a hand-drill.

'What fun!' he thought, and began to turn the handle.

Almost before he knew what was happening, he had drilled a small hole in the cupboard. It looked so neat that he drilled another, and then another, and another — until soon it looked as if woodworm had been at work. Patrick put the hand-drill away and went back into the house.

After tea, Patrick's father came into the sitting room looking very angry indeed.

'Who's been playing with my drill?' he asked.

'Not me,' said Patrick, for the third time that day.

But it was no use, his father knew Patrick was lying, and so did he. Patrick burst into tears.

'I'm sorry, Dad. I didn't mean to do it. And I didn't mean to tell lies,' he gulped.

His father stopped frowning, and gave Patrick a hug.

'Well, I suppose I'll forgive you!' he said. 'After all, you're not the first person who didn't mean to tell lies on Good Friday.'

Then Patrick's father told him all about Jesus' friend Peter who said he did not know him when Jesus was arrested.

'He felt awful because he thought he'd never see Jesus again, and he wouldn't be able to say "sorry". But then on Easter Day Jesus did come back again to see his friends.'

Patrick sniffed and rubbed his eyes.

'So the story had a happy ending, didn't it?' he said.

'Yes, and that's why we give each other Easter eggs on Easter Sunday,' explained his father. 'A real egg is the start of a new life; it hatches into a baby bird. In the same way, Jesus coming back was the start of a new life too.'

'So *that's* why we have to wait until Easter Sunday for Easter eggs!' said Patrick.

Activities

1   Read the Bible passages connected with the story: Jesus telling Peter that he would disown him (Matthew 26.30-35); Peter's betrayal (Matthew 26.69-75); Jesus' forgiveness (John 21.1-17).

2   A cock is mentioned in the Easter story. Throughout the ages, eggs have been used to symbolise new life — being born again. Show the children, and discuss, these drawings illustrating the development of a chicken from an egg.

Week 1   Week 3   Week 18

3   Decorate blown eggs, using a wide variety of materials, eg cotton wool, feathers, woodshavings, wool, glitter, coloured paper, crayons, felt-tipped pens.

To blow an egg:
   (i)   The egg must be at room temperature.
   (ii)   Prick the big end with a pin and enlarge the hole carefully.
   (iii) Make a hole in the small end.
   (iv)   Cover each hole with your fingers and shake the egg vigorously to break up the yolk.
   (v)   Hold the egg over a bowl or dish and blow hard through the smallest hole.
   (vi)   Leave the shell to dry out.

4   Make mosaics, using egg-shells which have been washed and broken into small pieces.

To make a mosaic:
   (i)   Pour different coloured vegetable dyes into saucers (very little is needed).
   (ii)   The children then put broken pieces of egg-shell onto the saucers to soak up the colour. (The egg-shells can also be painted before breaking.) Then they leave the shell to dry.

(iii) With glue, the children make patterns or outlines on paper, card or disposable plates, then sprinkle on the different coloured shell.

(iv) Leave to dry.

5 Organise an egg-rolling competition using hard-boiled eggs.

6 Make marzipan eggs.

Provide:
    115 gm (4 oz) ground almonds;
    225 gm (8 oz) sieved icing sugar;
    ¼ teaspoon almond essence;
    1 beaten egg.
    Or bought marzipan, ready to use.

Method:
(i) Put the ground almonds in a bowl, add the essence and icing sugar.

(ii) Add the egg a little at a time. Avoid making the mixture too wet. If it does become sticky, add a little sieved flour.

(iii) Knead.

(iv) Divide the marzipan into portions and dye with a few drops of different food colourings.

(v) Roll into miniature eggs and decorate with contrasting coloured pieces.

Simple baskets can be make by stapling handles to empty mousse or yoghurt containers. Line with crumpled tissue paper.

7 Make Easter cards. Talk about people who might like to receive them, and arrange delivery.

8 Do a project on the Romans.

(a) During Jesus' time, Palestine was just one part of the Roman Empire. Britain was another. Help the children to discover Roman Britain by studying Hadrian's Wall, and by finding out which roads and modern towns and cities have Roman origins.

(b) Teach the children the basic values of Roman numerals and how larger numbers are built up ($1=1$; $5=V$; $10=X$; $50=L$; $100=C$; $500=D$; $1,000=M$). Explain that the names of some of our months are named after Roman Gods (January — Janus; March — Mars; June — Juno).

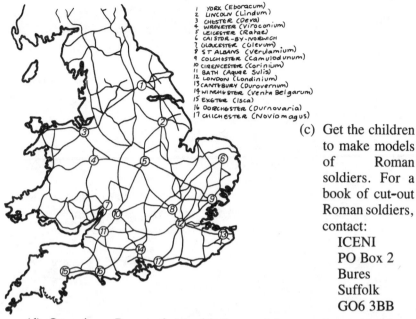

1. YORK (Eboracum)
2. LINCOLN (Lindum)
3. CHESTER (Deva)
4. WROXETER (Viroconium)
5. LEICESTER (Ratae)
6. CAISTOR-BY-NORWICH
7. GLOUCESTER (Glevum)
8. ST ALBANS (Verulamium)
9. COLCHESTER (Camulodunum)
10. CIRENCESTER (Corinium)
11. BATH (Aquae Sulis)
12. LONDON (Londinium)
13. CANTERBURY (Durovernum)
14. WINCHESTER (Venta Belgarum)
15. EXETER (Isca)
16. DORCHESTER (Durnovaria)
17. CHICHESTER (Noviomagus)

(c) Get the children to make models of Roman soldiers. For a book of cut-out Roman soldiers, contact:

ICENI
PO Box 2
Bures
Suffolk
GO6 3BB

(d) Organise a Roman feast with the participants wrapped in sheets (togas), reclining on their sides. Foods likely to have been eaten in this country in Roman times would have included fish, bread and porridge. This is an amusing way of learning about the practicalities of everyday life in Roman times.

(e) Many Roman coins bearing pictures of Caesar have been found over the years. Remind the children of the story in the Bible when the Pharisees tried to trick Jesus with a question about paying taxes and he answered by showing them a coin (Matthew 22.15-22). Then organise a coin-rubbing session.

Provide:

    as many different coins as possible;
    paper;
    wax crayons.

Method:

    (i)   The coin is placed on a flat surface (stuck down if necessary).

    (ii)   A piece of paper is help firmly over the top of the coin.

    (iii) Wax crayon is rubbed over the hidden surface of the coin.

Prayer

God, we are sorry that we do not always manage to live our lives as you would have us do.

Sometimes we break our promises,
        or we let people down,
        or we tell lies and are deceitful,
        or we say unkind things,
        or we physically hurt each other.

As we grow up, please help us to be aware of what's right and what's wrong, and help us to be able to say sorry when we should.

Hymn

1 When Jesus lived here on the earth and worked in Galilee,
some people rose and followed him but others said, 'Not me!'
'Not me, not me,' some people said, 'Not me, not me, not me.'

2 'Keep watch,' said Jesus to his friends while in Gethsemane,
but being tired they fell asleep. When challenged said, 'Not me.'
'Not me, not me,' his tired friends said, 'Not me, not me, not me.'

3 As daylight dawned and cockerel crowed the lies came, one, two, three.
When people said, 'You're Jesus' friend,' poor Peter said, 'Not me!'
'Not me, not me,' poor Peter said, 'Not me, not me, not me.'

4 On Easter day, after the cross, Jesus came back to see
his friends, and most of them believed, but Thomas said, 'Not me!'
'Not me, not me,' sad Thomas said, 'Not me, not me, not me.'

5 Although so many let him down, Lord Jesus hopes that we
will learn to love and follow him and never say 'Not me!'
'Not me, not me,' and never say, 'Not me! Not me! Not me!'

Words: Linda Hammond
Music: Traditional German Melody

Up early

We enjoy much more that happens around us when we use our senses to the full.

Up early

Marisha turned over in her sleeping-bag, and once more tried to get back to sleep. But it was no use — morning had arrived and daylight surrounded the little, white tent. As she lay there listening to the occasional burst of bird song in the unaccustomed silence, she thought about the day ahead. Although Marisha had never been to camp before, her brother, Leon, had told her all about it. He was a Scout and therefore considered himself an expert on such matters.

'You don't get any sleep,' he'd told her gleefully. 'And nobody makes you wash. It's great!'

Well, she'd had some sleep — and as far as washing was concerned, there was plenty of time for that.

Just then, Susan, the girl lying next to her, stirred.

'Are you awake?' Marisha whispered.

'No,' replied Susan, and she snuggled further into her sleeping bag.

'I am,' said Marisha. 'Have been for ages. In fact, I was thinking about getting up.'

'Well go on then,' muttered Susan. 'And stop bothering me!'

'All right, I will,' said Marisha.

So she put on some warm clothes, her anorak and her boots, and crept out of the tent.

It was so early that mist was still hovering around the campsite. The air felt fresh and cool on her face as Marisha walked slowly over the dew-soaked grass towards the washing block. There was no-one else about, but by the time she had finished using her flannel and toothbrush, a few of the others were beginning to get up. Soon the whole camp would be up, wanting breakfast. Marisha wandered over to the staff tent to see if there was anything she could do to help.

'Hello, Marisha,' said Mrs Roberts. 'You're up early! Did the birds wake you?'

'No,' replied Marisha. 'I woke up when it got light — and then I couldn't get back to sleep again.'

'Never mind,' said Mrs Roberts. 'Perhaps you'd like to go and see if the farmer has left us some milk.'

So Marisha set off across the wet grass once again, only this time she walked towards the gate at the far side of the field, arriving just in time to see the cows going past on their way to be milked. She was up early!

'Morning, love,' called the man who was driving them along the lane towards the farm. 'If it's the milk you're after, it's over there.'

He pointed to where several large, plastic containers were standing by the side of the road.

'They're heavy, mind. So no trying to carry them on your own,' he shouted over his shoulder as he followed the cows.

Marisha thanked him, and promised to get some help. Then she stood on the gate, watching and waving, until the man and his cows disappeared from sight.

When they had gone, Marisha climbed carefully down from the gate to go back to the camp, but as she did so, she noticed something shining in the hedge. Wondering what it could be, she ran over to have a look. There, hanging between the leaves, was a spider's web covered with dew, reflecting the rays of the early morning sun. It looked really beautiful to Marisha, who never usually noticed things like that.

When she got back to camp, breakfast was almost ready. She told Mrs Roberts about the milk and then went over to call Susan.

'Guess what!' she said. 'I saw cows going to be milked, and a beautiful spider's web . . .'

'So what?' interrupted her friend. 'I had an extra lie-in!'

'But you missed the morning,' Marisha told her.

'There's still more than enough of it left for me,' said Susan.

'But you missed such a lot,' Marisha thought to herself. 'I've never been up so early before and seen the day start. It was great. So if this is camping, I think I'm going to like it.'

Then the girls heard a whistle summoning them to breakfast.

'Let's sing grace before we start,' said Mrs Roberts, when they were all there, chattering and hungry.

Everyone fell silent. Then, very softly, the sound of singing drifted over the campsite . . .

'Thank you for the world so sweet . . .'

'And thank you for waking me early,' said Marisha, as she tucked into her cornflakes.

Activities

1 Read Genesis 1 to 2.3, for preference from Alan Dale's *Winding Quest*, pages 306-309. Ask the children what they think it would have been like on each of the seven days. For example, very, very quiet on the first day, etc.

2 Link this to Marisha's experience in the story when she woke up at camp and listened for sounds in the silence. Encourage the children to sit quietly for a few minutes and afterwards identify any sound they have heard.

3 Play a listening game.

Method:
   (i) All the children sit on the floor in a large circle round one child whose eyes are closed. (Pretending to be asleep.)
   (ii) A 'Marisha' is chosen. He or she tries to creep up and remove the sponge bag which is next to 'Susan' (the sleeping child) without being heard.
   (iii) If the sponge bag is removed without 'Susan' hearing, then another 'Marisha' is chosen.
   (iv) If 'Susan' does hear, then 'Marisha' becomes the sleeping guardian of the sponge bag while the old 'Susan' joins the others in the circle to continue the game.

4 Find out whether any of the children have ever been camping. Discuss, and display if possible, some of the items needed.

5 Ask the children to draw spiders' webs. Provide wool, glue and scissors, so that they can then build up their pictures if they want to. Talk to the children about spiders and the pests they eat. Explain that spiders should be encouraged.

6 Explain, using a torch or sunshine and a mirror, why the spider's web was shining in the story. Then shine light through a prism and show the children the refraction of light. Ask them to tell you what colours they see — red, orange, yellow, green, blue, indigo and violet. Let them paint their own rainbows.

7 Do a project on cows and dairy produce.
   (a) Using a blackboard for visual recording, see if the children can tell you the story of milk — from cows to cornflakes.

(b) Find out how many nursery rhymes and poems the children know which mention cows, milk, or something connected with them. For example, 'Little Boy Blue', 'Little Miss Muffet'.

(c) If possible, arrange for the children to visit a farm to watch cows being milked. Depending on your local area, this could be a country farm or a city farm.

(d) Follow this (again, if possible) with a visit to a dairy, so that the children can see what happens to the milk and how it is put into bottles.

(e) By now it should be well-established that we get milk from cows, but do the children know what we get from milk? Show them butter, cheese, yoghurt and cream. Taste and discuss.

(f) Encourage the children to collect and bring in labels from different dairy products so that they can be displayed.

(g) Make butter.

Provide:
  the cream from two pints of Gold Top milk;
  a saucepan;
  a clean, see-through, glass jar with a screw-on top;
  a *washed* wooden or plastic bead.

Method:
  (i)   Warm the cream to 40°C either directly over heat or by standing the jar in a saucepan of warm water. Do not overheat.
  (ii) Pour the cream into the glass jar, if not already done.
  (iii) Add the wooden or plastic bead. Screw the lid on tightly.
  (iv) Hand the jar over to the children to shake/churn the milk into butter. This will probably take about 40 minutes, so they will have to persevere.

Prayer

Father God, we thank you for giving us eyes
      so that we can appreciate the beauty and stillness
      of the early morning,
            and see spiders' webs sparkling in the sunshine.

We thank you for giving us ears
      so that we can hear the sounds of birds singing,
           and cows mooing on their way to be milked.

We thank you for giving us noses
      so that we can breathe in the cool, fresh air,
           and smell bacon cooking.

We thank you for giving us skin
      so that we can feel breezes, sunshine and wet grass.

We thank you for giving us mouths
      so that we can taste and enjoy what we eat and drink.

We thank you for giving us everything.

Hymn

1   Glad that I live am I,
    that the sky is blue;
    glad for the country lanes,
    and the fall of dew.

2   After the sun the rain,
    after the rain the sun;
    this is the way of life,
    till the work be done.

3   All that we need to do,
    be we low or high,
    is to see that we grow
    nearer the sky.

      Words: Lizette Woolworth Reese
      Music: Geoffrey Shaw

Martin the Monster

Living alongside people with different abilities and disabilities should be part of our daily lives. Different experiences and perspectives can stop us being narrow-minded and selfish.

Martin the Monster

Martin was a monster. From the time he got up in the morning to the time he went to bed nothing was ever right. If his Mum put out cornflakes for breakfast, he'd want porridge; if she asked him to put his coat on, he'd say 'No' because he'd be too hot; and if she told him to put all his toys away, he'd say 'Why should I?' and leave the room.

Things were not much better at school. When other children were asked to do things by the teacher, Martin would say 'It isn't fair' and whisper nasty things about them behind their backs. At dinner time he would always try and push his way to the front of the queue, and he never said sorry if he bumped into people.

So you can see that Martin really was a monster — a big, bad, horrible boy. But one day he changed and this is how it happened.

Every year, during the summer term, the children were taken on a school outing. This year it was to the seaside, and the big, red double-decker bus was nearly full by the time Martin the Monster arrived. He desperately wanted to go upstairs, and was very disappointed when he was told there was no room.

'It's not fair,' he grumbled as he took his place inside. 'Why should they all be up there and not me?'

The hour's journey to Brineborough passed quickly enough, and within minutes of arriving all the children were happily playing on the beach. Even Martin changed into his swimming trunks and seemed to be trying to enjoy himself. He picked up his bucket and wandered casually down towards the sea looking for shells.

'Hey, watch where you're walking, you great, clumsy elephant,' said an angry voice.

Martin stopped. Who was daring to speak to him like this?

'It's all right for you,' the voice continued. 'You can move out of the way, but I can't.'

Martin looked up, and found himself a few inches away from a wheelchair. For once in his life, Martin was speechless. It was true, he'd been so busy looking for shells that if the boy in the wheelchair hadn't called out, Martin would have walked straight into him and maybe knocked him over.

'Well, I didn't see you,' mumbled Martin.

'I know that,' replied the boy. 'But I didn't fancy lying on the sand for hours and hours.'

'You wouldn't have had to stay there,' said Martin, hurriedly. 'I'd have helped you back into your chair.'

'It's not as easy as that,' the boy told him. 'I can't move my legs at all — and my arms and hands only a little bit. On top of that I'm quite heavy, so you wouldn't have been able to lift me.'

'Are you here all on your own?' Martin wanted to know.

'No, my aunt and uncle brought me here,' said the boy. 'But they've gone for a cup of coffee. I told them I'd be all right. Mind you, that was before you came clomping along!'

Martin grinned. He was beginning to like this boy who was able to stand up for himself.

'Tell you what,' he said. 'How about if I stay and keep you company until your aunt and uncle get back?'

'Fine,' agreed the boy in the wheelchair. 'As long as you promise not to knock me over.'

As the minutes passed, the boys chatted. Martin told his new friend about all the things he did at school: reading; writing; looking after the guinea pigs; going out to play; helping at assembly; playing games. And never once did the other boy say 'It's not fair', even though he would never be able to do most of the things Martin mentioned.

Instead he said, 'Aren't you lucky? Mind you, I might be able to beat you at table tennis. I'm the champion of the class this year.'

'You probably would,' Martin agreed. 'I'm hopeless!'

And they both laughed.

Just then, the boy's aunt and uncle came back, so Martin got up to go.

'Have these shells,' he said, emptying the bucket onto the boy's lap. 'I can always get some more — and they might remind you of that great, clumsy elephant you once met on the beach.'

'Thanks a lot,' said the boy. 'I hope you don't forget me either, but I'm afraid I've got nothing to give you.'

'Don't worry about that,' replied Martin. 'You've made me realise just how much I've got to be thankful for. I shan't forget you in a hurry.'

'Good,' said the other boy with a grin. 'Just make sure you don't!'

Activities

1   Read and discuss some of the healing miracles of Jesus: the paralysed man, Luke 5.17-26; two blind men, Matthew 9.27-31; the man with a paralysed hand, Matthew 12.9-14.

2   Talk to the children about what happens today if people are ill. Show them how to use a telephone properly — taking the dial right round to the bottom or pressing the buttons firmly and slowly. Emphasise that they should always ask before using the telephone, except in an emergency. Explain what this is and what you should say if you have to dial 999.

3   Discuss all aspects of home safety: unused medical supplies; fires without guards, toys on stairs; pan-handles sticking out; etc. Then ask each child to make an 'Advent calender' type chart showing some of these potential hazards.

4   Do a project on disability, being sensitive to the feelings of any disabled children present.

   (a) Show the children pictures of disabled people. Discuss what it might be like to be disabled, for example to be blind, deaf, dumb or paraplegic. Talk about the help available: guide dogs; braille; hearing aids; wheelchairs; toilets for the disabled; special parking facilities for disabled drivers; etc.

   (b) Get the children to hunt through old newspapers to find articles about disabled people which can then be cut out and mounted for display.

   (c) Arrange for a disabled person to visit the class and talk to the children about his or her disability and how it is managed.

   (d) Try and find something practical for the children to do to help, even if it's only collecting milk bottle tops and tin foil for the blind.

   (e) Make a 'feeling' bag so that the children have to identify the articles placed in there by touch alone.

72

(f) Similarly, only this time using noses instead of hands, blindfold a few children and see if they can identify by smell objects or substances offered to them, for example an orange, chocolate, vinegar.

(g) Set up a obstacle course which the children have to tackle without using their hands and arms.

5 Provide each child with a large sheet of paper so that they can make charts of their daily activities, from getting up to going to bed.

6 Make a simplified class record of the activities involved in a school week.

7 In the story, Martin told the boy in the wheelchair that he helped to look after the guinea pigs. If your school has any pets, discuss their care.

8 Undertake a class survey to find out what are the most popular pets.

Prayer

Dear God,
sometimes we are like the old Martin:
> we grumble about the food we are given to eat,
> the clothes we have to wear,
> the things we are asked to do.

Sometimes we say 'It isn't fair'
> and talk about people behind their backs.

Sometimes we push in and don't wait our turn.

Sometimes we don't say sorry if we hurt people.

Sometimes we are not really at all the sort of children
> you would like us to be.

Please help us to change like Martin did,
> and to realise just how much we have got to be thankful for.

Hymn

1 God be in my head, and in my understanding;
God be in mine eyes, and in my looking;
God be in my mouth, and in my speaking;
God be in my heart, and in my thinking;
God be at mine end, and at my departing.

Words: Book of Hours
Music: Walford Davies

Shepherd for a day

A good shepherd cares for all his sheep, not just the majority who are easily found and looked after.

Shepherd for a day

One bright, sunny morning, while Sam was staying at his uncle and aunt's farm, Uncle John invited him to help round up the sheep.

'The sheep are brought back to the farm to be sheared ever year at about this time,' his uncle said. 'This means their warm, woolly winter coats are cut off so that they don't get too hot during the summer and so that we can sell the wool.'

Aunty Sue packed up a picnic lunch for them, which Uncle John put in his rucksack, along with some rope and a knife. He then whistled up Toby, his sheep-dog, and they set off across the fields towards the distant hills. Sam found it a long walk, but Uncle John was used to it. Toby kept running ahead, barking, and then coming back as if to ask why they were taking so long.

After about half an hour, Sam saw some white spots on the far hillside.

'Those are my sheep,' Uncle John said.

Toby began to get quite excited, and seemed most put out when Uncle John decided to stop and have lunch. While they were eating, Uncle John told Sam about rounding up the sheep.

'Toby does most of the work,' he said. 'I only watch what is happening, and give Toby instructions by using different whistles.'

When they had finished their meal, Uncle John stood up, looked around, and then gave a long, low whistle. Toby appeared as if from nowhere and immediately ran towards the sheep. Just before the dog reached the sheep, he slowed right down and started to move round the outside of the flock. One by one, Toby rounded the sheep up. Then, following Uncle John's whistled instructions, he guided them in a bunched up huddle towards the pen. As they ran into the pen, they were counted.

'One, two, three, four, five . . .' intoned Uncle John, until there were 48.

But there should have been 50, so where were the other two? Uncle John gave yet another, different sort of whistle, and once more Toby ran off up the hillside. Sam watched him sniffing the ground and looking under bushes. Then he stood absolutely still, with his head cocked on one side, listening hard. Suddenly, without warning, he began to run, and completely disappeared from sight.

Sam wondered where he had gone.

'Has he found the missing sheep?' he asked.

Uncle John signalled to him to stay quiet. A few minutes later, Toby was back, barking for Uncle John to follow him. Sam and Uncle John climbed round the side of the hill after the dog, and suddenly they came upon the sheep, standing on a rocky ledge. Uncle John had to use the rope he had brought with him to rescue the sheep, which was quite a business. It took so long, if fact, that Toby got tired of waiting and went off looking for rabbits!

Sam went after Toby, but he needn't have worried. One long whistle from Uncle John soon brought him back. Then they were all ready to drive the flock down the hill and back to the farm. This was no easy job, and it took all three to stop the sheep from wandering off and getting lost again. At last they reached the farmyard and the sheep were put into more pens for the night.

Uncle John gave Toby a big, juicy bone, as a thank-you for all his hard work. Then he and Sam went into the farmhouse to tell Aunty Sue all about their day.

Activities

1   Ask the children if they know why sheep and shepherds were talked about so much in Biblical times. Get them to tell you any stories on the subject they can think of, for example the Christmas story. Read Psalm 23 and the parable of the good shepherd (Luke 15.1-7), and encourage the children to think of modern equivalents.

2   Do a project on sheep.

   (a) Identify some of the main sheep-rearing areas in Britain — the Highland and Border regions of Scotland, the Welsh mountains, the Lake District, Dartmoor, Exmoor, Romney Marshes, the Downs — and explain the differences between them and the predominantly arable and dairy farming regions in other parts of

76

the country. Find out what sort of sheep (if any) are farmed round your area.

(b) Ask the children if they know what meat we get from sheep — lamb and mutton — and what the difference is. Discuss meat-eating and vegetarianism. If the class includes vegetarians, care will need to be taken that the conversation is not offensive to them.

(c) Wool is another by-product of sheep rearing. Talk about the way it is obtained, and the various methods used to make things from it, for example, spinning, knitting and weaving. Encourage the children to set up a wool interest table.

(d) Let each child make his or her own board picture.
Provide:
    small cork/polystyrene/wooden boards;
    hammers;
    nails/tacks/pins;
    wool.
Method:
    (i)   Carefully supervised, the children hammer nails part-way into the boards.
    (ii)   They then make patterns or pictures by threading the wool round the nails.

(e) Use 'Baa, baa, black sheep' and other nursery rhymes to encourage an awareness of rhythm — the children clapping or tapping on the beat. Sustain interest by making shakers.
Provide:
    (i)   A variety of clean, empty, plastic containers, for example yoghurt pots, margarine tubs, and squeezy bottles.
    (ii)   Dried beans, peas, bran, lentils, rice, sand, small stones, buttons.
    (iii)   A few short lengths of dowelling to use with the squeezy bottles.
    (iv)   Non-toxic glue, spreaders, sticky tape, cardboard, scissors.
    (v)   Paint, crepe paper, etc, for decoration.

Method:
- (i) Each child selects a container.
- (ii) The dried beans, peas, etc are put inside the container.
- (iii) The containers are sealed in the most appropriate way, for example: dowelling glued into the necks of the squeezy bottles; two yoghurt pots taped together; actual or cardboard lids glued or taped onto margarine tubs.
- (iv) The shakers are decorated if required.

When the children have finished, suggest they listen to the various shakers in turn and try to identify what is inside each.

3   If the children want to see a real flock of sheep they will have to visit the country, therefore it is important that they know how to behave. Introduce and explain the Country Code, which is as follows:

Guard against all risks of fire.
Fasten all gates.
Keep dogs under proper control.
Keep to paths across farmland.
Avoid damaging fences, hedges and walls.
Leave no litter — take it home.
Safeguard water supplies.
Protect wildlife, wild plants and trees.
Go carefully on country roads.
Respect the life of the countryside.

4   Although certain wild flowers have legal protection (encourage the children to find out which ones), grasses do not. Instigate a grass treasure hunt, with each *different* specimen being preserved in a scrapbook. If you have a good reference book, try to identify some of the grasses with the children.

5   Use dried or pressed grasses and flowers for a wide variety of craftwork — collages, notebooks, calendars, bookmarks, etc. Do *not* encourage the picking of wild flowers as a preliminary to this exercise.

6   Play a picnic basket memory game. Let the children watch as you put picnic items into a basket. Secretly remove something, then ask one child to look into the basket and identify what is missing. Repeat.

Prayer

Thank you, God,
for the beautiful world in which we live . . .
for blue skies, sparkling seas, snowcapped mountains, rolling hills, green
fields, domestic animals like sheep and cows, wild animals like foxes and
badgers, brightly coloured birds, insects and flowers.
(If possible, include suggestions made by the children.)

Thank you, God,
for caring about the world and all the creatures that live in it, no matter
what they do or how silly they are.

Thank you, God,
for sending your son, Jesus, to live amongst us so that he could show us
the right way to live.

Hymn

1 The gentle shepherd leads his sheep
    where pleasant pastures grow,
    and down the valleys dark and steep
    to cooling streams that flow.

79

2 They are so precious in his sight
that, when the day is done,
and they are brought to fold at night,
he counts them one by one.

3 And if one little frightened sheep
were lost upon the plain,
he'd go through valleys dark and steep
to bring it back again.

Words: Vivienne Sage
Music: S Stanley

Bike trouble

Prejudice is an ugly word and an ugly thing. Every person is different and should be accepted for what he or she really is.

Bike trouble

Home to Ben was a big block of flats which towered above a tangle of streets lined by little terraced houses. The houses and flats were filled with a hotch-potch of people, young and old, black, white and brown. Ben's father had little good to say about the black people, or the brown ones. And he had given Ben strict instructions not play with black children.

Not that that mattered to Ben too much, because there were always other things to think about. What Ben was thinking about most of the time was whether he would get a new bike for his birthday. His bike was long past its best and unable to do the necessary 'wheelies' and 'kick backs' which were required if you wanted to be part of the gang. He knew there wasn't much money at home, but a certain look in his mother's eye when bikes were mentioned had raised his hopes.

Day after day he pestered his parents for a new bike. At last, on his birthday, they gave in. Ben was over the moon, and couldn't wait to try out his wonderful new bike with its shining chrome handlebars and red wheels.

'Thanks a million!' he said as he gave his mother and father a big hug each.

After breakfast, Ben took his new bike downstairs in the lift. He wheeled it proudly to the road. Remembering what the policewoman had told him during his training for the Cycling Proficiency Test, Ben made sure nothing was coming before he mounted and wobbled off.

He was going to see his friend Steven, who lived a few streets away. It was still quite early in the morning, and there weren't many people about. He rode past the grocery shop, where Mr Aziz was out washing the steps. He rode past old Mrs Johnson, who was struggling to the grocer's pulling her shopping trolley. Then he reached the corner of the next street — and found his way ahead blocked.

Three very big, very rough boys were standing in the road with their arms held out to stop him riding past. Over by the grocery shop, Mr Aziz and Mrs Johnson were watching, shaking their heads angrily, but they were afraid to interfere.

'Get off that bike,' said a tall boy who looked as if he were trying to sound tougher than he felt.

Ben was scared, but he suddenly felt very angry as well. So he turned his bike slightly to ride round the bullies. One of the other boys, who had greasy hair, reached out and pushed him off the bike.

Ben didn't have time to put out an arm to break his fall, and he felt a shock of pain as his head hit the pavement. From somewhere, he could hear a little girl shouting. With a painful effort, he turned his head slightly, and saw two children running towards him. In a moment, the little girl was standing in front of the youths.

'Just you wait till I tell your father, Joe Carter,' she said, pointing at the tall boy.

He shuffled his feet and looked rather ashamed, then turned and went off down the road. The other two stood for a moment, then shrugged their shoulders, turned and followed him.

The little girl knelt down beside Ben. He saw that it saw Ruth, who sat near him in class. Ruth had clear, dark-brown skin and big, bright brown eyes, and she always came top in arithmetic.

'You mustn't move,' she said. 'My brother's just gone to fetch our dad. He's a doctor, so he'll look after you.'

Ruth's brother, David, fetched his father very quickly. Doctor Thomas was soon kneeling beside Ben, gently examining him for broken bones.

'I think you're all in one piece, young man,' he said. 'But we'll have to check you out at the hospital and keep you in overnight in case of concussion. Ruth, you and David take Ben's bike to our house for now, and I'll take him to the hospital.'

Ben felt sick and dizzy as Doctor Thomas lifted him gently into the back of the car, but he was worried that his parents wouldn't know where he was. He whispered his address to the doctor, who promised to go and see them as soon as Ben was settled in the hospital.

Next morning, when Ben woke up, feeling much better, his parents were sitting by his bed. They told him that they were taking him home as soon as he had had his breakfast, and that he would have a very special late birthday tea that afternoon.

It certainly was a special tea. When Ben saw all the cakes and sandwiches and the big bowl of trifle with whipped cream on top, he wondered how the three of them were going to eat it all.

He didn't have to wonder for long. The doorbell rang and his mother rushed to open the door. In came Ruth and David, Doctor Thomas, and a pretty lady who looked a bit like a grown-up Ruth.

Everybody was a bit shy at first, but they all enjoyed the delicious food so much that they soon began to chat more easily. Ruth, David and Ben sat on the floor and played games. The two mothers exchanged cake recipes, and Ben's father and Doctor Thomas talked about fishing. Before long, the two men had arranged to go fishing together the following weekend. When the others heard, they decided that they would all go for a picnic on the common on the same day.

'We can take our bikes,' said David, and the others eagerly agreed.

All too soon, it was time for the Thomas's to go home. It was the first of many, happy times the families spent together.

Activities

1   Read the parable of the good Samaritan in Luke 10.30-37. Compare it with the story and discuss.

2   Depending on age, ask the children to write or act a 'Good Samaritan' story.

3   Ruth, David and their father were kind and went out of their way to help Ben. Ask the children to think of some people whose jobs involve helping others. Talk about the work done by doctors, nurses, the police, etc, and (if possible) invite one or more of these people to come and meet the children.

4   Spotlight the West Indies, where Ruth and Simon's family originally came from. Include geographical location, crops, exports, food, carnivals, etc.

5   Make the point that every single person is different. What a person looks like is no way to judge their character. Play a game in which the children group themselves according to various criteria (*not* skin colour), for example:

blue eyes	brown eyes
short hair	long hair
likes sport	doesn't like sport
straight hair	curly hair
wearing glasses	not wearing glasses

over a certain height　　　　under a certain height
left-handed　　　　　　　　right-handed

Let the children see for themselves that the groupings are different each time.

6   Do a project on road safety.

(a) Introduce the children to, or remind them of, the Green Cross Code, emphasising that light controls on a pelican crossing are for *pedestrians*.

　　　　When the red man is shown　STOP
　　　　When the green man is shown　 GO

Ask the children to draw and colour one of each.

(b) Traffic using the road also has to obey lights which tell *drivers*, not pedestrians, when it is safe to go. Teach the children the sequence of the traffic lights, then play the following game to increase their powers of observation and their ability to react quickly.

An adult representing a set of traffic lights stands in the centre of the room, while the children 'drive' round. He or she then adopts one of the following three arm positions, which have to be obeyed immediately. The last child to do what is required is out.

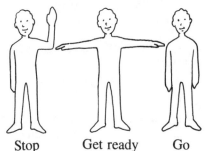

Stop　　　　Get ready　　　　Go

(c) Ask the children to make their own Highway Codes — to include rules for both pedestrians and cyclists and some road signs. Compare with copies of the real Highway Code.

(d) Invite the local Road Safety Officer to come and talk.

(e) Show the children a bicycle, name the different parts and talk about the importance of maintenance. If several members of the class own bicycles, then arrange for them to train and take a Cycling Proficiency Test, if they haven't already done so.

(f) Children need to know where they are going if they are to be safe out of doors.

　(i)　Show the children how to read an Ordinance Survey Map.

(ii) Suggest they draw maps of the area, including their own homes, schools, churches, shops, etc.

(iii) Teach them the points of the compass and show them how to get their bearings.

Prayer

Dear God, sometimes there is trouble at school,
>children quarrel,
>start fights,
>and are mean and unkind to each other.

Help us not to turn the other way
>and pretend it has nothing to do with us.

Help us to be like Ruth and David,
>who risked being attacked themselves
>when they went to see what had happened to Ben.

Please make us brave enough to help those in trouble
>and give us the courage the say and do what we think is right.

Hymn

1 When I needed a neighbour
   were you there, were you there?
   When I needed a neighbour, were you there?
   And the creed and the colour and the name won't matter,
   were you there?

2 I was hungry and thirsty, were you there . . .

3 I was cold, I was naked, were you there . . .

4 When I needed a shelter, were you there . . .

5 When I needed a healer, were you there . . .

6 Wherever you travel, I'll be there . . .

   Words and music: Sydney Carter

It happened to Hezron

Jesus chose ordinary workmen to be his disciples, men who caught fish for a living.

It happened to Hezron

Young Hezron turned over on his pallet and stretched himself. He could see a shaft of light penetrating the dark room and knew it would soon be time to get up. As he lay there, he wondered what the day ahead had in store for him. He loved the excitement of anticipating the unknown. To him, each day was an adventure, so the sooner it started the better.

He rolled off the straw pallet, and then began the daily search for his sandals. They were never where he thought he'd left them!

When his mother saw Hezron was up, she asked him to go and look for his two uncles, Simon and Andrew, who were fishermen. They had promised last night to be back with their catch in time for breakfast, but as yet there was no sign of them.

Hezron made his way through the narrow streets, towards the Lake of Gennesaret. Although it was still early, the sun already felt warm on his head, and he was glad to feel the gentle breeze blowing off the water.

He looked along the beach. There in the distance was his uncle's boat — but that wasn't all. There was a huge crowd. Something was up. Perhaps one of his uncles was in trouble. Hezron began to run, past nets and baskets piled high on the beach, jumping over ropes and then weaving his way in and out of the masses of people who were hurrying towards the far end of the beach. What on earth was going on? As he got nearer, he tried to see, but he wasn't tall enough. He jostled forward with the crowd, but he still couldn't see; and when he asked what was happening, he kept getting the same answer, 'It's Jesus! It's Jesus!', which didn't mean much to him. Jesus — which Jesus?

There was only one way to find out what was happening for himself. He stripped down to his loin cloth, paddled out into deeper water and then started swimming towards the boat. He was a good swimmer, so it didn't take him long to get within reach of the boat, which by this time was no longer beached, but was floating a little way off from the shore.

He could see his Uncle Simon sitting at the back, and another man, whom he didn't recognise, standing in the bow talking to the huge crowd which was still gathering along the water's edge.

Hezron tapped his uncle on the arm, gave a cheeky grin and then clambered all wet and dripping into the boat.

'Where's our breakfast?' he asked. 'Or have you stopped fishing and started taking passengers instead?'

And he pointed to the man at the front.

'Be quiet, you young vagabond,' his uncle replied, tweaking affectionately at his nephew's ear. 'Listen to what this man is saying and then I'll tell you about breakfast!'

Sitting behind him in the bobbing boat, Hezron and his uncle heard clearly what Jesus said to the crowd. He spoke in such a way that all could understand him and were eager to learn more. Even Hezron and his Uncle Simon, who were well known for their high spirits, listened spellbound. Who was this man?

When he had finished talking, Jesus turned away from the crowds and sat down to rest in the boat.

He then said to Simon, 'Put out into deep water and let down your nets for a catch.'

'Master, we were hard at work all night and caught nothing at all,' answered Simon. 'But, if you say so, I will let down the nets.'

So Simon and Hezron did what had been suggested and they made such a big haul of fish that their nets began to split. Frantically, Simon signalled to his partners, James and John. They came over in another boat to help. Soon both boats were loaded to the point of sinking.

When Simon saw this, he fell down on his knees in the bottom of the boat in front of Jesus.

'Go, Lord, leave me!' he said. 'I'm a rough and unworthy man!'

'Don't be afraid,' answered Jesus. 'From now on you will be catching people!'

'They won't taste very nice for breakfast!' thought Hezron, though he, too, was very impressed by what he had seen.

He wished he could do magic like that. But was it really magic? Jesus didn't look like a magician or a conjuror.

Hezron assumed that his uncles would be coming back for breakfast, as soon as both boats were safely back on the beach, especially as there was now plenty of fish to eat. But he was wrong — his uncles had changed. Jesus had offered them the chance to become 'fishers of people'. This meant helping him with his work, which was telling people all about God, and they were glad to take on the challenge.

Uncle Simon asked Hezron to tell his mother what had happened, and to ask her to forgive them for not going back. He then gave Hezron a huge basket of fish, a final tweak on the ear, and — telling him to be good — he set off with Andrew, James and John to follow in the footsteps of Jesus, along the beach.

Activities

1   Read the story of the full fishing nets in Luke 5.1-11. Compare with the story of Hezron and discuss.

2   Choose children to be Simon, Andrew, James and John, and allow them to run around with imaginary fishing nets, trying to catch people. Only let this go on long enough to make the point. Then introduce the children to the real meaning of Jesus' words.

3   Design and execute a class frieze on 'It happened to Hezron'.

4   Do a project on fish and fishing.

(a) The sign of the fish was one of the earliest symbols used to identify Christians. Suggest the children draw some things which could be symbols and write their associated meanings next to them.

For example: = baby   = school

(b) Buy or borrow a couple of goldfish for the classroom, so that the children can watch the fish swimming about.

(c) Ask the children if they think they could live underwater like a fish does, and if not, why not. Then explain that we cannot live underwater because we breathe by taking oxygen out of the air through our lungs, whereas fish take oxygen out of the water through their gills. Show how a candle burns oxygen from the air by lighting a candle in a jam jar and putting the lid on. The candle goes out when it has used up all the oxygen in the air.

(d) Ask the children to tell you the names of any fish they know —
fresh-water and salt-water. Arrange a visit to either a fish market,
a fishmonger, or the fish counter in a local shop.

(e) Talk about the different ways there are of catching fish. Start by
describing the way Jesus' disciples fished with a drag net, one end
of which would be attached to the shore and the other to the boat.
(For more details, see *Getting to know about farming and fishing*,
Brian Pitman, published by NCEC). Get hold of a rod and a net
to show the children how people in this country fish today.

(f) Play a fishing game.

Provide:
>   paper;
>   pencils and crayons;
>   scissors;
>   paper clips;
>   a container;
>   a rod make from a stick, string and a magnet.

Method:
- (i) The children all draw, colour, name and cut out some fish.
- (ii) A paper clip is attached to the mouth end of each fish. The fish are then put into the container.
- (iii) Each child then takes it in turn to try and catch fish using the magnetic rod.

Prayer

Jesus, we know you lived here on earth a long time ago.
>   When we hear stories like the one we have just heard,
>>   we feel as if we were there, like Hezron,
>>>   watching you talk to the crowds
>>>>   and seeing the nets all bulging with fish.

Please help us to feel you near us,
>   all the time,
>>   not just when we are thinking specially about you
>>>   in assemblies,
>>>>   in church,
>>>>>   or when we pray.

Hymn

1 Oh, he sat in the boat and he spoke to the crowd.
Haul, haul away.
And his voice wasn't soft and his voice wasn't loud.
Haul, haul away.
And he spoke of the just and the pure and the free,
and his voice caught the air like a net in the sea.
And it's haul, haul away. Haul, haul away.
Cast the nets wide and sink the nets deep and it's haul, haul away.

2 He said: 'Cast your nets wide where the water is deep.'
Haul, haul away.
'Oh, cast the nets wide and sink the nets deep.'
Haul, haul away.
'Though we've worked through the night and we've nothing to show,
we will try once again just because you say so.'
And it's . . .

3 Oh, the catch it was huge and the boat it was small.
Haul, haul away.
His friends came to help when they heard Peter call.
Haul, haul away.
'You must leave us,' said Peter, 'for we're men of sin.'
But he said: 'Come with me and be fishers of men.'
And it's . . .

Words: Michael Cockett
Music: Kevin Mayhew

BIBLE READINGS

HYMNS — first lines

ACTIVITIES